Historic Buildings & Landmarks of Dodge City

TIM WENZL

Photographs by Gentry Heimerman

Published with the assistance of grants provided by the
Community Foundation of Southwest Kansas
and Mariah Fund, Inc.

2

Contents

Preface, Acknowledgments

Dodge City is a town with an exclusive heritage. The community is well aware that its legacy is a valuable asset to be guarded and shared. Each generation understands that with Dodge City's historic legacy comes the responsibility of stewardship.

In 1976, the City of Dodge City approved an ordinance to establish the Landmark Preservation Committee to identify and protect the city's cultural heritage by designating certain buildings and structures as historic landmarks. Originally there were eight designated landmarks. That list has only grown; other buildings and sites are now included on the Register of Historic Kansas Places and the National Register of Historic Places.

When Dodge City's downtown area was listed as an Historic District on the National Register of Historic Places in 2009, it was recognized as a "distinct district with a visible sense of time and place." The Historic District includes twelve blocks of historic buildings constructed in the late nineteenth and early twentieth centuries.

In 2022, during the community's sesquicentennial, the City of Dodge City broke ground to revitalize the historic downtown area with a multi-million dollar streetscape project. The investment was designed to breathe new life into the downtown district to attract and accommodate new visitors and new businesses. The two-year project called for the creation of a central plaza, new landscaping, street lamps, additional public art, together with upgrades in infrastructure, parking, street design and walking paths.

Dodge City continues to experience a cultural renaissance. There is a spirit here that one can feel. Walk the streets and you'll find Western art in sculptures and murals. Art in public places is now a hallmark of the community. Is it any wonder that Dodge City was named "Best Summer Vacation Destination in the state of Kansas" in 2023?

A book project of this type requires a good team.

I am indebted to Gentry Heimerman, my photographer. I work with Gentry at the chancery office of the Catholic Diocese of Dodge City. He uses his skills in photography and videography in his position as Director of Young Adult Ministry. When I told him about this project and that I needed a good photographer, he was excited about the opportunity. He captured the beauty of brick and mortar, stone, bronze and paint and produced unique aerial shots with his drone.

I'm grateful to Nancy Jo Trauer, a native of Dodge City currently living in Hutchinson, Kansas, for writing the introduction to this volume. The subject of this book is very close to her heart. Nancy served on the city commission from 1974 through 1978 and was the city's first female mayor (1975-76). She served on the Dodge City Landmark Preservation Committee for thirty-five years. She is also a retired Director of the Dodge City Convention and Visitors Bureau.

I am grateful for the research materials at the Kansas Heritage Center and the assistance provided by John Mason, Jacque Orebaugh and Stephanie Birney. They were instrumental in locating photographs and articles from newspapers and fielding my many, many research inquiries. Research may be their job, but they went above and beyond in providing source material that enabled me to connect dots and fill in the blanks.

I am very grateful to Cynthia Vierthaler of the *Spearville News* in Spearville, Kansas, for her work in page design. She "quilted" patches of text and digital photographs to bring these pages to life. She also designed the book's cover.

I am most grateful to my editor Joyce Suellentrop of Prairie Village, Kansas, retired professor of History from Newman University. Her suggestions added value to the text and enriched each page.

I am especially grateful to the Community Foundation of Southwest Kansas and the Mariah Fund for the grants that made this project possible.

Tim Wenzl
May 10, 2023

Introduction

by Nancy Jo Trauer

The land in and around present-day Dodge City was once treeless horizons and rolling hills with buffalo herds and nomadic Native American tribes.

A section of the future town, located north of the Arkansas River and west of the 100th Meridian, was part of the 1803 Louisiana Purchase. The land south of the river, at various times, was claimed by Spain, France, Mexico and the Republic of Texas before it became part of the United States in 1848.

The Santa Fe Trail, a commercial freight route established in 1821 between Independence, Missouri, and Mexico, cut through the lands occupied by the Native Americans. As the tribes saw their livelihood threatened, they fiercely objected to the outsiders. In an effort to protect the traders and travelers, the United States government constructed a series of forts.

General Grenville M. Dodge ordered the creation of an additional fort southwest of Fort Larned to increase the military presence along the Santa Fe Trail in 1865. The site for the fort was chosen by Colonel James H. Ford, for whom Ford County is named, and was located on the Arkansas River several miles east of old Fort Atkinson. (see page 84) Colonel Ford named the military post, Fort Dodge, in honor of General Dodge. [1]

In 1871, Henry Sitler, a government contractor, built a sod house on the western edge of the military reservation as a headquarters to supply wood, hay and building stone to the fort. Because of its location on the Santa Fe Trail, the sod house became a popular resting spot for buffalo hunters and traders.

A major factor influencing the location of a settlement outside the military reservation was the prohibition of whiskey at Fort Dodge. George Hoover, a liquor dealer, left the fort with his wagon of whiskey and measured off five miles to the western boundary of the reservation. Dodge City's first business was a make-shift saloon that predated the town's existence.

Travelers on Santa Fe Trial, the buffalo trade, and activities at Fort Dodge, all influenced Dodge City's beginnings. The extension of the Atchison, Topeka and Santa Fe Railway through the area in 1872, however, led to the establishment of the town. At first, the businesses were nothing more than tents. Later, merchants constructed wooden buildings with false fronts, a trademark of frontier towns. [2]

On August 15, 1872, a town company formally organized and registered a plat of eighty-seven acres. The original settlers dubbed the town, "Buffalo City," due to the tremendous buffalo trade. However, an application to establish a post office as "Buffalo City" was denied upon discovering there was a "Buffalo, Kansas" in Wilson County. The town company then chartered under the name Dodge City.

It is generally thought the town took its name from Fort Dodge. However, Robert Wright, the first president of the town company, documented that the town, "Dodge City," was named to honor Colonel Richard I. Dodge. The Colonel was the fort's commander at the time of the town's organization and a leading town company military member. [3;4]

When the Dodge City Town Company organized in 1872, the settlement had no law enforcement except being under the jurisdiction of Ellis County, 100 miles to the north. After Ford County was organized in 1873, county officials hired a sheriff.

Between June 1872 and July 1873, eighteen killings are documented as well as eleven non-fatal incidents, though other unrecorded incidents are probable. "Boot Hill" burial numbers grew and Dodge City's reputation soon spread as "The wickedest little city in America." [5]

When the town incorporated on November 2, 1875, town officials hired officers of the law and passed ordinances. Some of the more famous Dodge City lawmen were Wyatt Earp, Bat Masterson and Bill Tilghman.

The Dodge City Town Company platted the town with a Front Street on either side of the railroad tracks. South of the tracks became known as "no man's land" due to lawless events prevalent there. In an effort to establish a semblance of order, city officials passed a city ordinance prohibiting the carrying of firearms north of the tracks.

Buffalo hunting became Dodge City's first major industry. Hunters flocked to the region following the area's tremendous herds. The town became the largest shipping point in the country for buffalo hides and meat. After four years the buffalo were decimated, halting a lucrative buffalo product shipping business.

Dodge City may have wasted away on the plains had it not been for cattle drives from Texas. Drovers annually herded Texas Longhorns to shipping points at Wichita, Abilene, and Ellsworth. Then it was discovered the Longhorns carried a tick for splenetic fever and while Texas cattle were immune to the disease, they caused wide spread devastation among Kansas herds.

In 1876, the Kansas Legislature protected local cattle ranchers by enacting legislation for a quarantine line west of the major existing shipping markets. The line banned Texas Longhorns from entering east of the line. As a result, drovers herded Longhorns to Dodge City, establishing a major railhead here. In 1875, 250,000 head were driven from Texas to Dodge. After the 1876 quarantine line legislation, the numbers steadily grew, and the town became known as "Queen of the Cowtowns."

Dodge City enjoyed the longest cattle era of any of the Kansas cowtowns. The Kansas quarantine law of 1885, however, prohibited Texas Longhorns from entering the state altogether and the community was dealt a blow when the cattle trails no longer led to Dodge.

Rough times got rougher when fires destroyed many of Dodge City's businesses in 1885 and 1886. Things only got worse when a blizzard in 1886 destroyed local herds leaving the town's local cattle industry crippled.

All was not lost however. Even before the Longhorn drives ceased, settlers moved into the region establishing farms and ranches. Dodge City businesses rose from the ashes building back with brick structures. The late 1880s through the early 1900s were marked by community service developments for water and sewer systems, telephone and street paving projects. The tough times only strengthened the spirit of the town's founders and the early settlers and there was a revival of economic growth.

From the beginning, economic conditions dictated Dodge City's evolution. These conditions, along with the area's cultural and aesthetic values, created the community's spirit and shape of today. Dodge City stands as a tribute to tenacious frontier settlers, and later citizens, who contributed to its growth.

Historic Buildings and Landmarks of Dodge City records very well the community endeavors and the vision of Dodge City's residents to preserve its heritage.

'Welcome to Dodge'

Travelers approaching Dodge City on the highways from east and west are welcomed to the community by two metal sculptures depicting cowboys on horseback silhouetted against the horizon. The sculptures evolved as a project of the Dodge City Area Chamber of Commerce 1996 Leadership Dodge Class. Greg Gaskill of Gaskill Build/Design facilitated the project. The east sculpture, top, was installed in 1998; the west in 2002. The west sculpture was removed in 2022 pending highway construction.

Landscape Architect: Roger Sherman, BHA Design of Fort Collins, Colorado.
Sculptor/Fabricator: Lowell Tasset, Tasset Machine & Iron Works
Stonemason: Gary Esquibel, Dodge City

District One

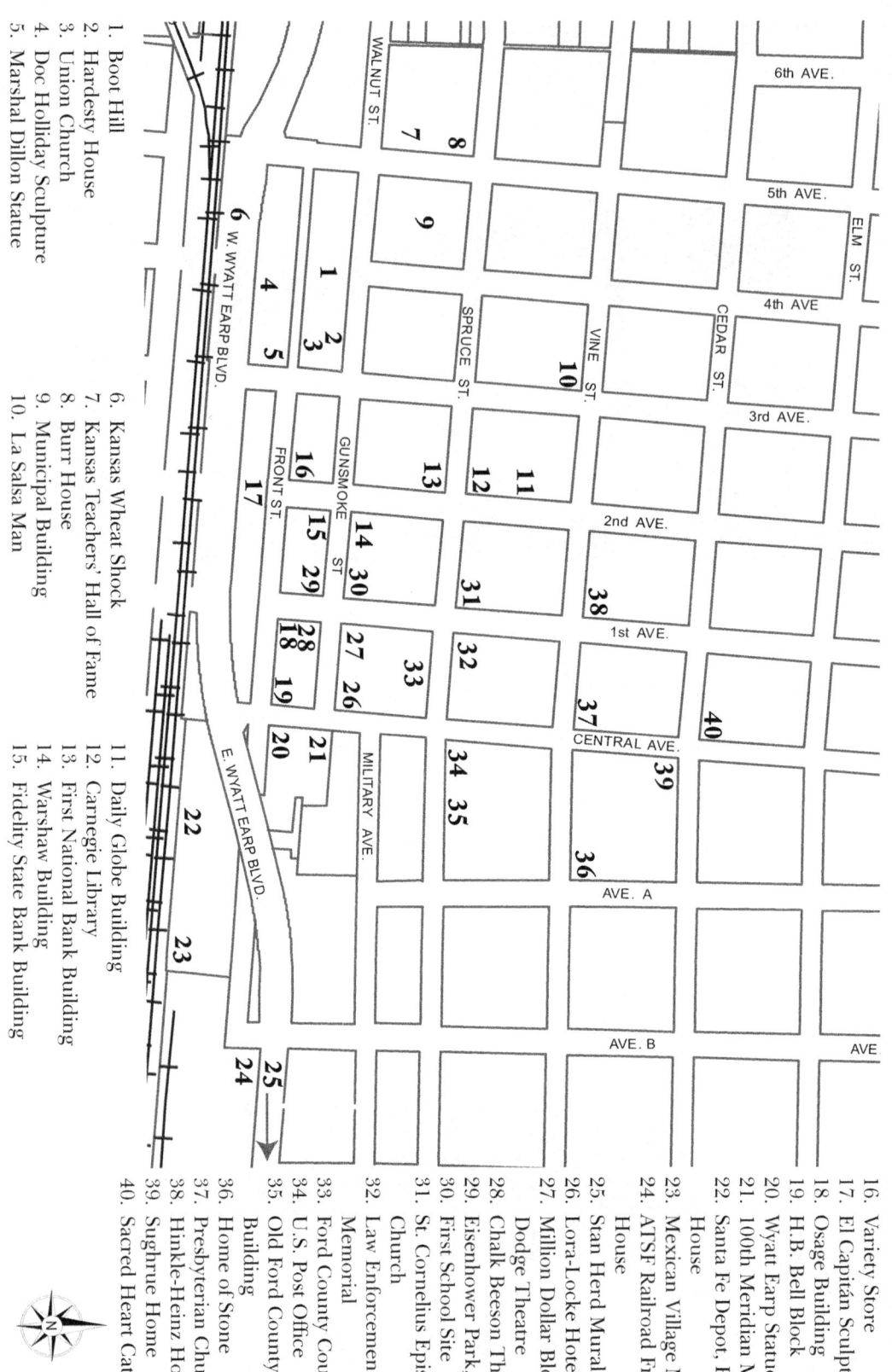

1. Boot Hill
2. Hardesty House
3. Union Church
4. Doc Holliday Sculpture
5. Marshal Dillon Statue
6. Kansas Wheat Shock
7. Kansas Teachers' Hall of Fame
8. Burr House
9. Municipal Building
10. La Salsa Man
11. Daily Globe Building
12. Carnegie Library
13. First National Bank Building
14. Warshaw Building
15. Fidelity State Bank Building
16. Variety Store
17. El Capitán Sculpture
18. Osage Building
19. H.B. Bell Block
20. Wyatt Earp Statue
21. 100th Meridian Marker
22. Santa Fe Depot, Harvey House
23. Mexican Village Marker
24. ATSF Railroad Freight House
25. Stan Herd Mural Panels
26. Lora-Locke Hotel
27. Million Dollar Block,
28. Dodge Theatre
29. Chalk Beeson Theater
30. First School Site
31. St. Cornelius Episcopal Church
32. Law Enforcement Officers Memorial
33. Ford County Courthouse
34. U.S. Post Office
35. Old Ford County Health Building
36. Home of Stone
37. Presbyterian Church
38. Hinkle-Heinz House
39. Sughrue Home
40. Sacred Heart Cathedral

8

Boot Hill - Front Street Complex 1

Cemetery: 1872-1878
Public School Site: 1878-1927
Municipal Building: 1929[6]

The hill west and north of the Front Street business district was a burial ground for unfortunates for six years after the establishment of Dodge City in 1872. Those killed by gunmen who had neither money or friends were interred here. Persons dying in Dodge City who had friends, relatives or money received a proper burial at the Fort Dodge cemetery.

Boot Hill was never the official city cemetery. The burial site started during the town's wild and notorious days out of necessity. Located close to Front Street where many met their demise, the dead were buried on the hill wherever it was convenient. They were buried with their boots on; some with boots crossed behind their heads for a pillow. Thus the name "Boot Hill" came into being and spread throughout the Western frontier.

The name was applied to frontier cemeteries in a number of communities with a more or less notorious history. The number of graves on Boot Hill is estimated to have been at least thirty.[7]

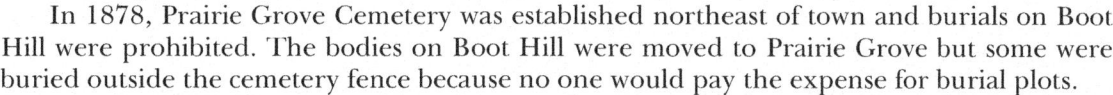

In 1878, Prairie Grove Cemetery was established northeast of town and burials on Boot Hill were prohibited. The bodies on Boot Hill were moved to Prairie Grove but some were buried outside the cemetery fence because no one would pay the expense for burial plots.

Shortly after the bodies were moved, construction for a two-story brick schoolhouse was initiated. This building served as the city's elementary school from 1880 to 1890. The growing student population led to the construction of a larger school on the same site. This school served the community until 1927 when it was razed to make way for the construction of the municipal building.

On November 4, 1929, a grand celebration was planned to mark the laying of the cornerstone for what would be Dodge City's second city hall. Civic leaders publicized and organized festivities for what was billed as "The Last Roundup." The event drew 25,000 people to Boot Hill. Frontiersmen, pioneers, cavalry soldiers, Civil War veterans and cowboys, all of whom played a role in settling the plains, reunited and joined in the festivities. The dedication of Dr. O.H. Simpson's cowboy statue was the highpoint of the event. (see page 21)

When Dodge City hosted the Kansas Rotarian convention in 1932, the legendary Boot Hill became a tourist destination. Dr. Simpson, wanting to provide a little amusement, created mock graves for the occasion. The graves consisted of wooden markers, concrete death masks and boots which were half buried in the soil. After the convention, the display remained and drew many curiosity seekers. The following year, Dodge City hosted a convention for the Kansas Lions Clubs. Dr. Simpson created a steer heads monument that added to the display.

By 1936, the popularity of the exhibition led to the hiring of William "Dad" Rhodes as caretaker-custodian. A canvas tent was erected and a booth set up with a register and for the sale of souvenirs. Rhodes boasted that the register was signed by more than 12,000 people in two days during the premiere of the 1939 movie *Dodge City*. He served as Dodge City's ambassador on Boot Hill for more than a decade.

When Rhodes retired in February of 1947, an article in the *Dodge City Daily Globe* included these paragraphs:

"The future of Boot Hill is uncertain.

"No plan has been advanced as yet for keeping the landmark open to tourists...

"Whether or not Boot Hill will be continued as an historic bit of western lore to attract thousands of travelers to Dodge City depends on future development. Those who pass that way today will find it deserted, with much of its color gone.

"Since 'Dad' Rhodes left, there's no one to tell its story." [8]

To say the article caused a stir in the community would be a gross understatement. The Junior Chamber of Commerce (the Jaycees) accepted the challenge and ideas flourished for a "Boot Hill improvement project." On March 26, 1947, just a month after Rhodes' retirement, ground was broken for a building that served as the first Boot Hill Museum. The Jaycees added a collection of interesting and historical items and Boot Hill Museum soon became a storehouse of relics of the old Southwest. [9]

Over the years, ideas developed for the construction of a Western town as part of Boot Hill. On January 27, 1958, Hugh O'Brian, star of the television series *The Life and Legend of Wyatt Earp* (1955-1961), assisted in laying the cornerstone for the Front Street Replica. The

10

Circa 1954

replica (below) is an authentic reproduction of the center block of Front Street as it appeared around 1876. O'Brian also took part in the ceremonies officially changing Chestnut Street to Wyatt Earp Boulevard.

After the replica was constructed, the family of Chalkley Beeson, donated approximately 5,000 artifacts from its Beeson Museum that had operated in south Dodge City since 1932. [10] The collection included exhibits, artifacts and photographs of the early years of Dodge City and southwest Kansas.

In 1964 and 1971, additional buildings were constructed at the Front Street Replica. The grounds have been enhanced by the donations of structures that include a Victorian home, a railroad depot, and a country church.

A new 3,000-square foot museum building was completed in 2021. The structure includes a lobby, a gallery for traveling exhibits, educational presentations and special events, additional exhibit areas, a gift shop and a covered patio for guests to watch entertainment in the shade.

Circa 1963

Summertime entertainment includes reenactments of frontier gunfights by the Boot Hill Gunfighters and performances by Miss Kitty and the can-can dancers in the Long Branch Variety Show.

The Boot Hill Museum complex is one of the top tourist attractions in Kansas drawing visitors from throughout the United States and many foreign countries. The collections at the museum include over 20,000 artifacts. It is listed on the Register of Historic Kansas Places.

2023

2023

The Kansas Cowboy Hall of Fame

The Kansas Cowboy Hall of Fame is located within the Boot Hill - Front Street Complex in an original museum building. Each year since 2002, Kansas cowboys and cowgirls are nominated for their contributions to the western heritage lifestyle.

Honorees are recognized in five categories: Working Cowboy, Rodeo Cowboy, Rancher/Cattleman, Cowboy Historian and Cowboy Entertainer/Artist.

A statewide Kansas Cowboy Hall of Fame Committee meets annually to consider nominations. After the induction ceremony, the honoree's photo and biography are displayed in the exhibit. Each inductee is said to personify the traditional cowboy values of integrity, honesty and self-sufficiency. [11]

13

Hardesty House   2

Hardesty House, a Victorian Gothic Revival villa with bay windows and gingerbread verge boards, was constructed in 1878 by A.B. Webster of Dodge City. It was designated as a city landmark by the Dodge City Landmark Preservation Commission in 1977.

The home bears the name of Colonel R. J. "Jack" Hardesty, who was one of the richest pioneer ranchers in the West. The Kentucky-born Hardesty made his first fortune in the gold fields of Montana and then invested in cattle.

Hardesty, in partnership with his brother John, had large cattle herds in Texas, New Mexico, Oklahoma and Kansas. Hardesty's Half Circle S Ranch in the Oklahoma panhandle was the major base of operations. Two thousand five hundred head of cattle were branded at this location each year alone. [12]

Hardesty was a major supporter and organizer of the Dodge City Cattle Growers Association, which later became the Western Kansas Cattle Growers Association. The town of Hardesty, Oklahoma, was named for him.

The Hardesty residence was one of the early showplaces in Dodge City. Hardesty often sponsored grand parties in his home. The Christmas ball was considered the social event of the year. [13]

Colonel Hardesty lived in the house from 1880 until he died in 1910 at the age of 77. His funeral was held in the parlor of the home.

The Hardesty family sold the house in 1916. The home was occupied as a family residence until 1969. When Skelly Oil Company purchased the lots in 800 block of West Wyatt Earp Boulevard, its original location, the structure was moved and presented to the Boot Hill Museum.

Union Church   3

Dodge City had a non-denominational church as early as 1876. That structure no longer exists, but the importance of the Union Church to the frontier community was recognized with the restoration of a church donated from Bucklin, Kansas, in 2008.

Originally an oil field shack, the structure was converted to a church in 1943 by Bucklin's fledging Catholic congregation. It was dedicated as St. George Church after the patron saint of the first pastor Msgr. George Husmann. The church served the congregation until 1991.

The structure now serves as a museum with photographs and artifacts from the congregations that originally worshiped in the Union Church. It is available to the public for worship services and weddings.

Doc Holliday Sculpture   4

A life-sized bronze statue of Doc Holliday, sitting at a poker table with three empty chairs, is an interactive sculpture inviting visitors to join the game. Holliday is poised with his hand reaching for his six-shooter for any cardsharps dealing from the bottom of the deck. The sculpture was created by Janet Zoble and cast by Deggingers' Foundry, both of Topeka, Kansas. It was commissioned by the Dodge City Trail of Fame and installed at the intersection of Fourth Avenue and Wyatt Earp Boulevard in 2015.

John Henry "Doc" Holliday practiced dentistry in Dodge City for a time, but his primary source of income was gambling. He had a reputation of being good with a gun and handling conflicts. Holliday is probably best known for his role in the gunfight at the O.K. Corral, assisting Vigil, Morgan and Wyatt Earp against a group of outlaws in Tombstone, Arizona, on October 26, 1881. Holliday died of tuberculosis November 8, 1887, at the age of thirty-six. He is buried in Linwood Cemetery overlooking Glenwood Springs, Colorado. [14]

Marshal Dillon Statue   5
400 West Wyatt Earp Boulevard

A life-size bronze statue of James Arness as U.S. Marshal Matt Dillon in the television series *Gunsmoke* stands at the Dodge City Visitor Center.

Gunsmoke aired from 1955 to 1975 with a total of 635 episodes. In addition to Arness, cast members included: Amanda Blake as Miss Kitty; Milburn Stone, as Doc; Dennis Weaver as Chester Goode; Ken Curtis as Festus Haggen, Buck Taylor, who played Newly O'Brian, gunsmith turned deputy; Burt Reynolds as Quint Asper, and Glenn Strange, as bartender Sam Noonan. These actors have been recognized with medallions on the Dodge City Trail of Fame.

(see page 32)

Dodge City is a pilgrimage destination for *Gunsmoke* fans. The city hosted 50th and 60th anniversary events for the television series in 2005 and 2015. Actors and writers from the show attended both celebrations.

The Marshal Dillon statue was created by Tony Cipriano of New York. Arness' widow, Janet, Buck Taylor, and Ben Bates, Arness' stunt double, were on hand for the unveiling July 30, 2017.

Gunsmoke exhibit at Boot Hill Museum

Kansas Wheat Shock Sculpture   6
Median, Wyatt Earp Boulevard

South of the Boot Hill Museum complex, prominently located in the median of Wyatt Earp Boulevard, is a thirty-seven-foot steel sculpture celebrating the importance of hard red winter wheat to the area. Kansas became known as the Wheat State in the early twentieth century when it became a leader in wheat production.

The sculpture was commissioned in 1983 to mark the 100th anniversary of the *High Plains Journal*, a weekly agricultural publication. Ted Carlson, the *Journal's* art director, sketched the design; Mark "Hoss" Haley, a local artist, was the sculptor. The Wheat Shock was originally located on the lawn of *Journal* building at 1500 E. Wyatt Earp Boulevard. After the publication moved its offices and sold the building, the sculpture was donated to the City of Dodge City in 2022.

The *Journal's* parent newspaper was established in 1883 under the flag *Dodge City Democrat*. In 1905, the name of the publication changed to the *Dodge City Journal Democrat*. It was known as the *Dodge City Journal* from 1909 to 1948. In 1945, the publication changed its editorial focus to agricultural news. The publication has been titled the *High Plains Journal* since 1949.

Brick Streets
Downtown Heritage District

Dodge City has more than fourteen miles of brick streets. The brick streets in the downtown area were paved between 1913 and 1916. They are protected as a contributing factor to the Downtown Historic District designation on the National Register of Historic Places.

The dark red paving bricks are more than two inches thick. They were burned from shale in Buffalo, Kansas. Beneath the brick roadway is a concrete base.

The bricks are set in a horizontal pattern from curb to curb. At the intersections, the pattern changes to a cross-diagonal weave. Although decorative, the weave was developed to insure heavy wagons, trucks and automobiles, would not dislodge the bricks during turns.

The Kansas Teachers' Hall of Fame   7
603 Fifth Avenue

The Kansas Teachers' Hall of Fame was chartered on February 15, 1977. It is the first such hall of fame in the United States. The purpose of the facility is to highlight the teaching profession and the many teachers who have dedicated their lives to help others become worthwhile and contributing members of society.

Outstanding Kansas teachers or administrators who have contributed at least twenty-five years to education K-12 are eligible for nomination. District Heads and the Board of Directors meet annually to evaluate nominations and select inductees.

The Kansas Teachers' Hall of Fame was first located in a one-room schoolhouse adjacent to the Front Street Replica. The Hall of Fame quickly outgrew the schoolhouse and relocated west of the Boot Hill complex at 603 Fifth Avenue in 1982. This building also houses the Gunfighters' Wax Museum. Behind the Hall of Fame is the restored Pleasant Hill School, a country school from Hodgeman County.

In 1978 the Kansas Legislature passed a resolution designating the first Friday in March of each year "Teacher Day." The idea for Teacher Day originated with Laurence Stanton, a member of the Board of Directors of the Hall of Fame. Stanton was inducted in the Class of 1980. He taught in Kansas schools from 1933 to 1974. His tenure at Dodge City Senior High School included positions of teacher, coach, athletic director, assistant principal and principal. Stanton saw his idea for Teacher Day develop into a national reality when President Jimmy Carter signed a proclamation designing March 7, 1980, as Teacher Day, USA.

Burr House   8
603 West Spruce

Burr House, one block west of Boot Hill, is a National Register property nominated for its architectural significance and its association with Hiram T. Burr, a successful Dodge City businessman and real estate developer.

Burr House was constructed between 1927 and 1928. The residence is unique as an example of the Dutch Colonial Revival architecture. Some of the significant features of the structure are the continuous dormer across the front, an entry portico with curved pediment, and a cross-gambreled roof.

Early in his career, Hiram Burr was the southwest Kansas district agent for the Connecticut Insurance Company. He later established Hiram T. Burr, Inc. a real estate, insurance and loan firm. He was known as a "modern builder of Dodge City" for his work in commercial and residential development.

Burr was also involved in community service. During World War I, he served in Dodge City's 16th Battalion of the Kansas State Guard. He was a member of the Dodge City Phoenix Industrial Club and hosted its meetings. The Phoenix Club was the forerunner of the chamber of commerce. Members met regularly to discuss business prospects and the social needs of the community while enjoying billiards and cards. [15]

The Burr family occupied the home until 1947. It remained a residence for several different families and was later utilized as an office for a real estate company. In 1994 the seven bedroom residence was converted into a bed and breakfast.

Municipal Building 9
501 West Spruce Street

Dodge City chose the prestigious Boot Hill as the location for its second city hall, the municipal building. The architect was Mann and Company of Hutchinson, Kansas; the builder was J.N. Parham of Dodge City.

A towering and ornately designed brick structure, located south of the railroad tracks, served the community as city hall from 1888 to 1928. When the building was razed the limestone carving of a buffalo head over the main entrance was salvaged. That sculpture was placed in the brickwork over the city marshal's entrance during the construction of the new building in 1929 and 1930.

The municipal building housed city offices, the municipal courtroom and judge's chambers, police department and the city jail. These departments relocated in 1965. The fire department continued to utilize the building until a new fire station was constructed at 201 Soule Street in 1995. The building has also been occupied by the Chamber of Commerce and the Convention and Visitor's Bureau.

In 2014, the structure became the home of Boot Hill Distillery. The building was renovated to include the distillery, located in the former fire department bays, a tasting room and cocktail lounge. The back and front bars from the historic Bill's Tavern are located in the tasting room. [16] The second floor, where the jail cells were located, and a back patio provide space for meetings and gatherings.

The Municipal Building was listed on the National Register in 2001. The lawn includes commemorative sculptures and monuments. (see pages 21-22)

Cowboy Statue, Yoked Oxen

Dr. O.H. Simpson, a pioneer dentist, retired from practice in 1923 and took up sculpture as a diversion. Simpson is best known for his cowboy statue and yoke of oxen in front of the municipal building.

The model for the statue was Joe Sughrue, a cowboy and later Dodge City Chief of Police from 1933 to 1936. Simpson identified Sughrue as "the epitome of the old time cowboy."

The concrete-reinforced-with-steel statue was created from plaster molds. Sections of Sughrue's body were covered with plaster of Paris, a substance used in the field of dentistry to mold dentures.

While covering the top part of Sughrue's body, Simpson provided Sughrue with a paper straw to breathe. At one point Simpson accidentally pinched the straw and Sughrue almost suffocated.

The statue was completed in 1927, but dedicated during "The Last Roundup," on November 29, 1929. The inscription on the statue's base: "On the Ashes of My Campfire this City is Built," was written by Lane Dutton, a Dodge City attorney and municipal judge.

The sculpture of the yoked Longhorn oxen was unveiled during a convention of the Kansas Lions Clubs in 1933.[17] The Southwest Historical Society, a predecessor of the Ford County Historical Society, furnished the bronze plaque that bears an inscription also penned by Dutton: "My Trails Have Become Your Highways, Seven Million Head of Longhorns Marketed from Dodge City, '70s – '80s." (see page 29)

In 2015, after overlooking Dodge City for eighty-six years, the iconic Cowboy Statue was restored by Pishny Restoration Services of Lenexa, Kansas. A time capsule with Dodge City memorabilia was placed in the base "only to be opened when the statue is in need of restoration again."

In addition to his hobby as a sculptor, Dr. Simpson is remembered for his contribution to the field of dentistry as the inventor of the gold inlay. When he needed thin gold plate for filling patients' cavities, Dr. Simpson would place gold coins on the railroad tracks to be flattened by a passing train.[18]

Ham Bell Monument

The monument to Hamilton B. "Ham" Bell honors one of Dodge City's most reputable citizens and incorporates the bell that rang in the community's first house of worship, the Union Church (see page 45). The Junior Chamber of Commerce erected the monument in 1939 as a drinking fountain for visitors to Boot Hill.

Ham Bell came to Dodge City in 1874 and made it his home until his death at the age of 93 in 1947. He served Dodge City as a businessman, civic leader and law enforcement officer. He was a farmer, rancher, ice manufacturer, livery barn operator, undertaker, furniture store proprietor, automobile dealer, realtor, mayor (1912-1915); sheriff of Ford County (1888-1911) and U.S. Deputy Marshal at various times between 1888 to 1892.

Bell is best remembered as the sponsor of an annual pioneer picnic held in Wright Park. The first Ham Bell Pioneer Picnic was a surprise party held on his birthday July 31, 1934. A group of friends started the event, but Bell continued the annual get-together. The summer celebration endured long after his death until 1976. The Ham Bell Picnic was reestablished by the Ford County Historical Society in 2022, during events marking the 150th anniversary of Dodge City's founding. Food, games, entertainment and history orations are included in the community event.

Dodge City Centennial Monument

After Dodge City celebrated its centennial year in 1972, an idea for commemorating the milestone emerged. DeRos Hogue, a Dodge City native, designed a monument with the centennial seal atop a tapered metal column. Four separate brick markers encircle the monument with informative plaques about the Boot Hill Cemetery Site, George M. Hoover, one of the town's founders (see page 60); Wyatt Earp, infamous law enforcement officer (see page 31); and L.W. Davis (see below).

L.W. "Dad" Davis Memorial

Leroy Wilson Davis served as a police officer from 1922 to 1943. When he died in 1944, one year after his retirement at the age of 84, a marker was placed on the lawn of the municipal building as a memorial. Davis was known for his good-natured tolerance in handling prisoners. He joined the police force when he was sixty-two where his twin sons, Leroy and Levi were already officers. His nickname, "Dad," grew out of the family ties within the department. The original memorial stone is incorporated in the centennial monument.

La Salsa Man 10
Third Avenue and Vine Street

La Salsa Man, a fiberglass sculpture standing twenty-six feet in height was donated to the Dodge City Area Arts Council by Dennis Hopper's art trust in 2012. Hopper, born in Dodge City on May 17, 1936, was a filmmaker, photographer and art collector. *La Salsa Man*, created by Bob "Daddy-O" Wade of Austin, Texas, toured the country with Hopper's art show. After suffering wind damage, *La Salsa Man* was restored in 2022 by Inga Ojala, an artist based in Bucklin, Kansas.

Hopper is best known for co-starring with Peter Fonda and Jack Nicholson in the 1969 movie *Easy Rider*. Hopper co-wrote and directed the film that received an Academy Award for Best Original Screenplay.

In 2022, the Ford County Historical Society commissioned Topeka artist Janet Zoble to create a life-sized sculpture of Hopper dressed in character as Billy astride the Harley-Davidson motorcycle he rode in *Easy Rider*. The sculpture will include room to join Hopper on the bike for a photo-op. (artist's conception below)

The murals behind *La Salsa Man* were painted by Stan Herd, a native of Protection, Kansas. The panels, depicting cowboys branding cattle on the range and a track crew laying rails across the prairie, were originally included in the panoramic mural wrapping the National Beef plant at 2000 East Trail Street. Several of the mural's scenes were relocated due to plant expansion. (see page 65)

Daily Globe Building   11
705 Second Avenue

This building was designed by Mann and Company of Hutchinson, Kansas, and constructed by Fred Lipps of Dodge City in 1926. It's original use was as a lodge for the International Order of Odd Fellows. It also served as a home for the Dodge City Commercial College, KGNO radio, the Gum Motor Company and a dance studio. After the newspaper moved its operations into the building in 1935, the brick storefront was renovated with stonework complete with "DAILY GLOBE" in Art Deco style. After occupying the building for eighty-seven years, the newspaper moved its offices in 2022. The new owner initiated renovations for commercial and office space.

Dodge City's newspaper has a lineage reaching back to the early days of the town's notorious past. The parent newspaper was established as a weekly publication in 1878 under the flag *Ford County Globe*. In 1884, the name changed to the *Globe Live Stock Journal*. In 1889, the *Journal* consolidated with the *Ford County Republican*, another weekly newspaper established in 1886, and the name changed to the *Globe-Republican*.

In 1910, the newspaper underwent still another step in its evolution. J.C. Denious, an ambitious thirty-one-year-old reporter with the *Wichita Beacon*, was convinced that the course of empire followed the development of transportation facilities. Denious decided to make his home where the railroad constructed the next branch line. In this way he could witness and play a part in the growth of a small community.

In the fall of 1910, Denious learned that the Atchison, Topeka and Santa Fe Railroad intended to construct a branch line southwest from Dodge City to Elkhart. He left Wichita, purchased an interest in the *Globe-Republican* and changed the name of the newspaper to the *Dodge City Globe*. On December 11, 1911, the name of the newspaper changed again with the birth of the daily edition, the *Dodge City Daily Globe*. J.C. Denious became the sole owner of the newspaper in 1914.

The newspaper remained in the hands of the Denious family until 1988. The publishers, in order of succession were: J.C. Denious (1910-1953); Jess Denious (1953-1969); Juliet Denious (1969-1973); and Martha Denious Muncy (1973-1988). Complimentary advertising for community events and non-profit organizations was standard practice for the newspaper.

Since 1988, the newspaper has been owned successively by Stauffer Communications, Morris Communications, Gatehouse Media, Gannet Company, and CherryRoad Media.

Carnegie Library 12
701 Second Avenue

Dodge City's Carnegie Library building was constructed between 1906 and 1907. The architect was C.W. Squires of Emporia, Kansas; the builder, William Foley of Dodge City. The structure is one of 1,679 public libraries constructed in the United States with the financial assistance of Andrew Carnegie, steel magnate and internationally known philanthropist.

The architectural style known as Beaux Arts is unique to this area. The building, with its corner entrance, visually commands the street intersection. A tiered dome covers the two-story drum. Bas-relief pediments surmounting the side walls and the Ionic pilasters flanking the entrance are Classical influences. Stained glass enhances the windows throughout the building. A west addition was constructed by the Works Progress Administration in 1936.

The Dodge City Public Library outgrew the structure and relocated in 1970. Over the next decade, the building housed restaurants and cafés named Red Palace, Casey Jones Junction and Kreme Kup; and nightclubs named fittingly, The Library, and Opera House 21.

The Dodge City Historic Preservation Committee first recognized the structure as a city landmark in 1977. The building was named to the Register of Historic Kansas Places and placed on the National Register in 1979. The Dodge City Area Arts Council initiated a drive to renovate the building in 1980. The structure was dedicated as the Carnegie Center for the Arts on December 6, 1981. The galleries are utilized for local and traveling exhibits as well as lectures, workshops and art classes.

The "Reading Garden" behind the Carnegie Arts Center is a fitting compliment to the building's former use as a library and a tribute to the Denious family that owned the *Dodge City Daily Globe* beside it.

First National Bank Building   13
619 Second Avenue

The skyline of Dodge City underwent a dramatic change with the construction of the First National Bank Building. When completed in 1930, the city had a "skyscraper."

The architect was Fred Organ of Omaha, Nebraska; the builder Eastergard and Bullard of McCook, Nebraska. The six-story brick and stone structure was designed in the Classical Revival style. The two-lower floors are distinguished by a stone facade with Corinthian pilasters and full height windows. The upper floors have tan brick with stone detailing.

The State Bank of Commerce was founded in 1901 when the organizers purchased the existing Midland Bank. In 1904, the name changed to the National Bank of Commerce. It became First National Bank in Dodge City in 1921. Due to a national trend of merging financial institutions beginning in 1994, the name changed to Bank IV, Boatman's Bank, NationsBank and Bank of America. The last financial institution to occupy the building left the community in 2015. An ownership group purchased the structure in 2021 with the intent to renovate it for residential and commercial space.

Stagecoach Mural

The mural on the south face of the First National Bank building was painted by Stan Herd, a native of Protection, Kansas, in 1979. It commemorates the stage as the most efficient means of passenger travel prior to the coming of the railroad.

The thirty-five by forty-five foot mural was fashioned after Frederic Remington's *The Old Stagecoach of the Plains*. A guard, atop the coach, poised with a rifle, watches for trouble and serves as a reminder of the dangers of traveling on the plains.

After the railroads were constructed for east - west travel, the stage lines became important as conveyance for north and south travelers and the U.S. mail. P.G. Reynolds operated the Dodge City and Panhandle Stage Line south into Texas, north to WaKeeney, Kansas, and southwest to New Mexico. The stage line was discontinued in 1888. [19]

Warshaw Building 14
600 Second Avenue

This one-story red brick structure has distinct design features. The corbeled cornice band around the two sides of this corner building is highlighted with white glazed brick. The west and south facades exhibit stonework with Art Deco detailing and lettering. The west entry is inscribed "WARSHAW."

Warshaw's was an upscale men's clothing store that operated from 1917 to 1996. The haberdashery, first located at First Avenue and Chestnut Street, relocated to 600 Second Avenue in 1930. The store's merchandise included Hart, Schaffner and Marx clothing, Stetson hats, Manhattan shirts, Bostonian shoes, Bradley sweaters, Crown work clothes and Beals and Selkirk luggage. [20]

The structure was originally occupied by the J.B. Byars Company, a national dry goods and ready to wear store. In 1929 Byars merged with J.C. Penney. The first J.C. Penney store in Dodge City occupied this building only a year before moving into larger quarters.

Fidelity State Bank Building 15
510 Second Avenue

Dignity and power, created in the use of Classical architecture, is revealed in banking institutions constructed in the early decades of twentieth century America. The Fidelity State Bank building exhibits a simple grandeur in the use of white enameled brick with terracotta trimmings and fluted Ionic columns flanking the main entrance.

Kansas State Bank built this structure in 1916. The architect was J. Carl Jourdan of Kansas City, Mo.; the builder was William Foley of Dodge City.

Fidelity State Bank was founded in 1932 with the merger of Kansas State Bank and the State Bank of Dodge City. Ben Zimmerman, Sr., began his career at Kansas State Bank in 1919. Operations at Fidelity State Bank have continued under four generations of the Zimmerman family.

Variety Store 16
501 Second Avenue

In 1885 and 1886, multiple fires destroyed the frame business structures along Front Street. What resulted was a brick building boom to "fireproof" the businesses.

This structure was constructed in 1887, and stands as the only remaining nineteenth century commercial building in downtown Dodge City. Despite the removal of the cornice, the existing upper facade portrays the buildings original character. [21]

Numerous retail businesses have occupied this building. The Williams Variety Store was a former tenant.

Circa 1986

El Capitán   17
Second Avenue and Wyatt Earp Boulevard

The impact of the cattle industry on Dodge City's economy is memorialized in the bronze Longhorn sculpture at Second Avenue and Wyatt Earp Boulevard. The sculpture, with a horn span of 100 inches, was created by Jasper D'Ambrosi of Tempe, Arizona, in 1981.

The importance of cattle and the railroad to the community prompted Lois Flanagan to enter *El Capitán* in a "name the Longhorn contest." Flanagan who served the community as assistant librarian from 1940 to 1951 and head librarian from 1951 to 1972, was greatly aware of the significance of both.

El Capitán, Spanish for "The Captain," is a befitting name for the Longhorn that established itself as the leader of the herd on cattle drives. Some drovers used the same steer over several years. The name was also a subtle tribute to the *El Capitán* passenger train operated by the Atchison, Topeka and Santa Fe Railway between Chicago and Los Angeles from 1938 to 1971. Dodge City was one of the stops along the route.

Between 1875 and 1885, seven million head of cattle were driven up the Great Western Trail from Texas and Oklahoma and shipped to eastern markets from the railhead in Dodge City. The sculpture faces south looking down the trail, now U.S. 283.

———————◆◆◆———————

Great Western Trail Marker

Adjacent to *El Capitán* is a concrete post marking Dodge City as a destination along the route of the Great Western Trail. The marker was placed by the Great Western Cattle Trail Association in 2004.

The Great Western Cattle Trail played an integral role in the development of Dodge City. As early as 1861 the Kansas Legislature enacted quarantine laws to keep Texas cattle from infecting Kansas cattle with a fatal disease known as "Texas Fever." Over time, the quarantine line that began in the eastern part of the state moved westward. In 1875, an amendment moved the quarantine line west of Wichita, Newton and Ellsworth, shutting down those railheads.[22] As a result, Dodge City became the primary railhead for the cattle drives. The cattle business, and the city's notorious reputation, grew over the next decade. By 1885, however, the quarantine laws were statewide and Dodge City was no longer a destination for the Texas cattle herds.

Osage Building   18
502 First Avenue

The Osage Building was constructed in 1928. The architectural firm was Mann and Company of Hutchinson, Kansas; the builder was J.N. Parham of Dodge City. The three-story brick building includes stone detailing around the storefronts and the entrance to the upper floor apartments. The upper facade is enhanced with arched brick arcades.

This business and apartment building was named for its proximity to what was the northwest corner of the 8,736,000-acre Osage Reservation. The Osage lands in Kansas encompassed an area defined roughly by eastern boundaries of what is today Labette and Neosho counties, west 273 miles to the 100th Meridian running south through Ford and Clark counties and back east along the Kansas-Oklahoma border to the point of origin. [23]

The Osage remained in Kansas until 1870, when the United States government, reacting to mounting pressure to open the prairie to settlement, passed legislation mandating their removal. At the insistence of the Osage, the government assisted in the purchase of land from the Cherokees in "Indian Territory." This land is now known as Osage County, the largest county in Oklahoma. [24]

H.B. Bell Block   19
110-114 West Wyatt Earp Boulevard

The 100th block of West Wyatt Earp Boulevard was occupied by what was commonly known as the Bell Garage. Hamilton B. "Ham" Bell constructed the building operating an automobile dealership and ambulance service from 1916 to 1924. The building was converted to commercial space with individual storefronts.

Wyatt Earp Statue   20
Central Avenue and Wyatt Earp Boulevard

The eight-foot tall bronze sculpture of famed lawman Wyatt Earp on the east edge of Dodge City's Historic District was created by Oklahoma artist Mary Spurgeon. The sculpture was designed to show motion. Earp is turning, with right hand on his buntline special and his frock coat flared out. He is seemingly responding to the sound of a voice or the cock of a revolver from someone on Front Street. Wyatt Earp was an assistant marshal in Dodge City from 1876 to 1879. The sculpture, the first commissioned by the Dodge City Trail of Fame, was dedicated November 12, 2004.

Trail of Fame
Throughout Historic Downtown

The Trail of Fame is part of a historic walkway throughout downtown Dodge City that includes numerous bronze medallions and statues. The twenty-four-inch medallions recognize historic figures from the community's colorful past, city founders, community advocates, and actors who portrayed characters in Westerns and television series. Statues of Wyatt Earp, Doc Holiday, James Arness as Matt Dillon, and Bat Masterson, are included.

The Trail of Fame was initiated in 2002 by a Downtown Dodge committee headed by Jim Johnson, a retired meteorologist with the National Weather Service. It was developed as "a living trail to bring history to life." The growth and success of the Trail of Fame prompted its transfer to the Ford County Historical Society in 2022. Medallion induction ceremonies and statue dedications are ongoing events. (see page 32)

Trail of Fame Inductees [25]

Actors from *Gunsmoke* Television Series (1955-1975)

James Arness (see Marshall Matt Dillion sculpture, page 16)

Ben Bates - Stunt double for James Arness

Amanda Blake - Miss Kitty Russell, owner of the Long Branch Saloon

Bruce Boxleitner - Guest appearances; Western actor

Ken Curtis - Festus Hagan, scruffy comedic deputy

Roger Ewing - Thad Greenwood, deputy marshal

James Nusser - Louie Pheeters, town drunk

Burt Reynolds - Quint Asper, blacksmith; deputy

Milburn Stone - Doc Adams, frontier doctor

Glenn Strange - Sam Noonan, bartender

Buck Taylor - Deputy Marshal Newly O'Brian

Dennis Weaver - Chester Goode, stiff-legged assistant to Marshal Dillion

Actors from Movies and Television

Gene Barry - Lead role in television series *Bat Masterson*, (1958-1961)

Errol Flynn – Sheriff Wade Hatton, 1939 Movie *Dodge City*

Henry Fonda - Portrayed Wyatt Earp in 1946 movie *My Darling Clementine*

Dennis Hopper - Actor, filmmaker, photographer (see page 23)

Hugh O'Brian - Lead role, *The Life and Legend of Wyatt Earp* television series (1955-1961)

Historic Figures

Hamilton "Ham" Bell - (see page 22)

Chalk Beeson - (see page 41)

Brig. General George Armstrong Custer - Calvary Officer, Cut wagon road from Fort Dodge to Camp Supply in present-day Oklahoma

General Grenville M. Dodge - Civil War general, railroad magnate, namesake of Fort Dodge

Wyatt Earp (see sculpture, page 31)

"Big Nose" Kate Elder - gambler and longtime companion of Doc Holliday

Fred Harvey - developer of Harvey House restaurants and hotels along the Santa Fe Railroad

"Doc" Holliday (see sculpture, page 15)

Ramon House - Dodge City's last official U.S. Marshal

"Bat" Masterson (see sculpture page 48)

T.L. McCarthy - Dodge City's Frontier Doctor

Charles Rath - owner of the Rath Mercantile Store, early outfitter for buffalo hunters

Community Advocates

Joe Bogner – Anheuser Busch wholesaler, philanthropist and community leader "Community is what makes us, so we need to give back to the community."

Lewis and Rosemary Mock - Dr. Lewis Mock founded the Long Branch Variety Show in 1958; he accompanied the singers and dancers on piano. His wife Rosemary portrayed "Miss Kitty."

Don Steele - founder of the Depot Theater Company, was instrumental in the restoration of the Santa Fe Depot

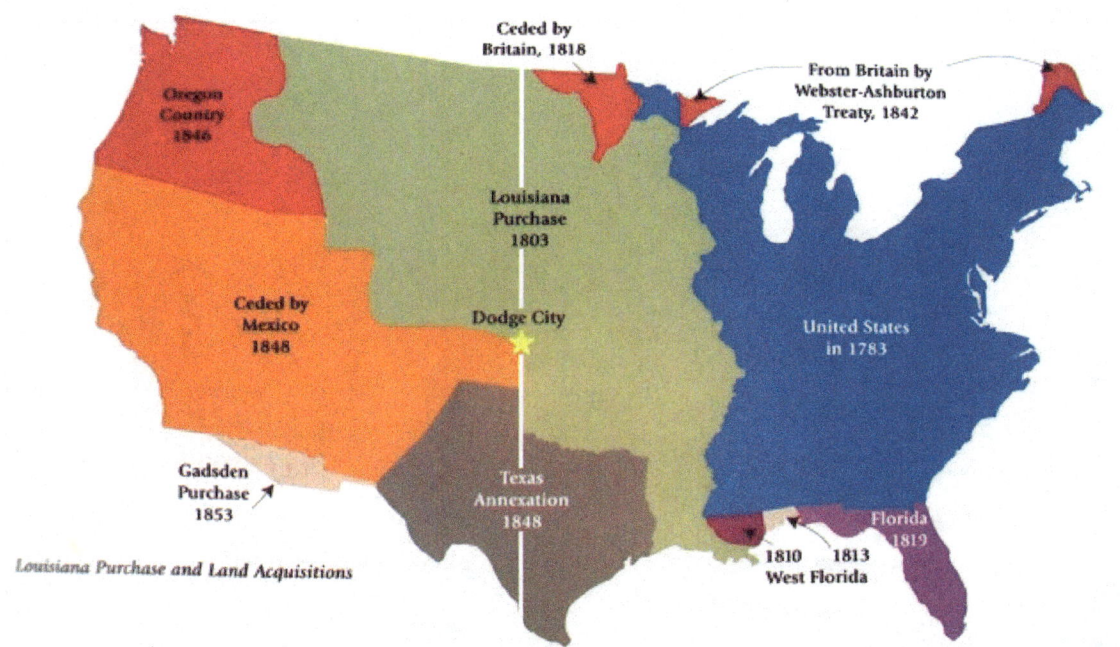

Ceded by
Britain, 1818

From Britain by
Webster-Ashburton
Treaty, 1842

Oregon
Country
1846

Louisiana
Purchase
1803

Ceded by
Mexico
1848

Dodge City

United States
in 1783

Gadsden
Purchase
1853

Texas
Annexation
1848

Florida
1819

1810   1813
West Florida

Louisiana Purchase and Land Acquisitions

100th Meridian Marker   21

Dodge City sits on the 100th Meridian, an imaginary geographic coordinate that stretches from the North Pole to the South Pole. While the 100th Meridian was historically an important detail in mapping boundary lines, its exact location through Dodge City has been elusive.

The 100th Meridian was used in establishing a corner of the boundary between the United States and Spain in the Adams-Onis Treaty of 1819. The eastern boundary of the lands claimed by Spain followed the 100th Meridian to the Arkansas River and then proceeded west. All of Dodge City south and west of this point was owned by Spain.

In 1825, George Champlin Sibley, surveying the Santa Fe Trail, thought the 100th Meridian was some nine miles west of present day Dodge City near the Santa Fe Trail Remains (see page 85). Samuel Smoot, surveying the Osage Ceded Lands in 1867, thought the 100th Meridian was near today's Matt Down Lane at the western edge of Dodge City. Another attempt to locate the 100th Meridian in 1935 placed it at Central Avenue running north through Dodge City. There was even a local legend that the 100th Meridian passed directly between the two giant sundials on the grounds of the Santa Fe Depot. (see page 35)

In 2007, the mystery of the location of the 100th Meridian in Dodge City was solved thanks to Michael Snapp, a Boy Scout from Troop 162 working on his Eagle project. Snapp enlisted the expertise of Kevin Noll of A to Z Land Surveying in Jetmore, Kansas. He and Vernon Bogart, a retired land surveyor, used a Global Positioning System to determine the 100th Meridian's exact location. Snapp carved a 600 pound limestone post with the words "100th Meridian" that sets between Avenues L and M on Wyatt Earp Boulevard. A storyboard detailing the historical significance of the 100th Meridian is located in the downtown area near the Wyatt Earp statue.

Santa Fe Depot, Harvey House Hotel   22
100 East Wyatt Earp Boulevard

The life of a frontier town depended on the railroad. Some towns flourished if they were "on the railroad;" others died if the railroad "missed them." In 1872, the year Dodge City was chartered, the Atchison, Topeka and Santa Fe Railway laid rails through the community. This was Dodge City's link to the East, first for marketing buffalo hides, bones and meat and later for marketing cattle.

A boxcar on a side track served the community as the first depot. In 1873, a frame depot was constructed at the foot of Central Avenue (then known as Railroad Avenue).

The present depot was constructed in 1897 and dedicated in 1898. The architect was J.C. Holland and Company of Topeka, Kansas; the builder was Fellows and Van Sant, also of Topeka. It is the largest depot still in existence in the state. It was placed on the National Register of Historic Places in 2000 for its historic significance in the growth and development of Dodge; its association with the Atchison, Topeka and Santa Fe Railway Company (ATSF); and its example of Richardsonian Romanesque architectural style.

The depot's heavy stone foundation, brick-masonry walls, stonework, round-topped arches, bands of windows, and tower are all hallmarks of Richardsonian Romanesque architecture.[26]

The red brick structure is trimmed in red cut stone from Colorado City, Colorado; the foundation stone is from Castle Rock, Colorado. The roof is covered with terracotta tile. The balconies at the north and south sides of the third story are made of pressed copper, thirty feet long by four feet in width.

The west room on the first floor housed the railroad office; the east side held the express and baggage rooms. Completing the first floor were ladies' and gents' waiting rooms a lunch counter, dining room, Harvey House hotel office, kitchen, pantry, bakery and refrigerator rooms. Located in the basement were the boiler room, root cellar, coal house, store room and laundry.

There were twenty-eight sleeping rooms and a ladies' parlor on the second floor, and five sleeping rooms on the third floor. The depot was expanded to accommodate more hotel rooms in 1909 and 1914. The Santa Fe Railroad gave the Harvey House its picturesque name, *El Vaquero* at the time of the 1914 expansion.

In 1925 another addition was constructed providing room for food preparation for the Harvey House operations as well as supporting the dining cars that Fred Harvey operated on the Santa Fe passenger trains.

El Vaquero was forced to close in 1948 after dining cars became standard on all transcontinental trains. Hotel rooms and a newsstand remained in operation into the mid-1950s. The hotel portion closed due to the growth of automobile travel and the decline of rail passengers.

The Burlington Northern Santa Fe Railway donated the depot to the City of Dodge City in 1996. The former hotel lobby is the main gathering room with many of the original fixtures, flooring, counter, woodwork and leaded glass windows. The Harvey House dining room has been restored for meeting and event space.

The east end of the depot is occupied by the Depot Theater Company and utilized for dinner theater and other live performances. A room on the second floor was restored by the Theater Guild to illustrate lodgings in the Harvey House Hotel.

The west end houses an area for Amtrak and the offices of Dodge City Public Transit, whose bus routes also serve the depot.

The second floor has been renovated to accommodate offices of the Dodge City Convention and Visitors' Bureau, Dodge City - Ford County Development Corporation, and the Dodge City Area Chamber of Commerce.

Twin Sundials

The 100th Meridian, passing through Dodge City, was the dividing point between the Central and Mountain time zones for the Santa Fe Railroad. Due to its geographic location, the Dodge City terminus was where the rail company changed time for the operation of its trains.

In 1897, after frequent questions about the time change from rail passengers, the twin sundials were constructed on the depot grounds in view of the train windows. Primarily ornamental, the sundials reminded eastbound travelers to move their watches up an hour and westbound travelers to move their watches back an hour.

In 1928, R.G. Whyman, a Santa Fe employee, had the sundials scientifically reconstructed for accuracy. Additional renovation projects took place in 1952, 1984 and 2003. Walter Thomas of Troop 168 refurbished the sundials in 1984 as his Eagle Scout project.

The sundials, with radial lines of twenty-four feet, include Roman numbers for the hours; the words Mountain and Central are along the forty-eight foot bases. The gnomons, the steel poles that create the shadows on the sundial faces, are supported by other upright poles twelve feet high.

Dodge City's sundials were featured in *The Mentor*, a New York magazine, in a 1917 edition that highlighted "the most famous clocks and other time pieces the world has known." [27] Another article featuring the sundials appeared in the August 1937 issue of *National Geographic*.

Circa 1928

1922

The grounds around the Santa Fe Depot were known as Railroad Park. In addition to the Sundials, flower gardens, and shade trees, the park included the Santa Fe Reading Room as a convenience for passengers waiting to board trains. The freight house, still in existence, is located at the far right.

The Sundials, are the last remnant of Railroad Park that bordered the depot on the north and east. The park, landscaped with trees and gardens, presented an oasis in stark contrast to the Kansas plains viewed for hours by the rail passengers. The rail company viewed the park as such an important asset that gardeners and custodians were hired to keep up its appearance. Henry Ikeda, a native of Japan, maintained the grounds from 1912 to 1947. [28]

Mexican Village Marker   23

A historical marker recognizing Dodge City's Mexican Village is located near the caboose in the southeast corner of the Depot Theater parking lot. The storyboard, dedicated on October 20, 2007, was a project undertaken by Eagle Scout Shane Scott of Boy Scout Troop 162.

The Mexican Village was a community of immigrant railroad laborers and their families. The community had a fifty-year history extending from 1906 to 1956 before the Village was closed and its residents relocated. (see page 43)

In 1933, the Village was populated by 401 people who lived in seventy-seven homes on five and a half acres. The Village included a grocery store, a dance hall, a pool hall, a grade school named for Coronado, and a Catholic church under the patronage of Our Lady of Guadalupe. [29]

An exhibit about Dodge City's Mexican Village opened at the Boot Hill Museum in 2023. The exhibit documents the community's history with murals, photographs and artifacts.

Mexican Village mural in the Boot Hill Museum exhibit.

ATSF Railroad Freight House   24
207 East Wyatt Earp Boulevard

The Atchison, Topeka and Santa Fe Railway constructed a new freight house two blocks east of the depot in 1913. The structure was converted for use as a restaurant in 1992. Three eateries have occupied the building: The Freight House, Steakhouse Depot & Restaurant, and Central Station Bar and Grill.

The ATSF freight offices were located in the two story brick structure. The frame warehouse, sheds and transfer platforms extended to the east. At the time of construction, the structure was lauded as the most modern freight house in Kansas.

The original wooden freight house, located south of the Santa Fe Depot, had been in use since 1873. When it was torn down, the lumber was used to build houses in the Mexican Village.

Stan Herd Mural Panels   25
301 East Wyatt Earp Boulevard

The mural panels on the Western Beverage building at 301 East Wyatt Earp Boulevard were originally included in the historical panorama painted by Stan Herd around HyPlains Dressed Beef in 1985. (see page 65) After the business was sold to National Beef, the facility was enlarged and sections of the mural removed. Joe Bogner, then owner and president of Western Beverage, obtained two scenes of the panorama. Herd painted a new center panel to combine the scenes. The scene at right was fashioned from Charles Russell's 1909 painting entitled *In Without Knocking*.

Lora-Locke Hotel
Ford County Government Center 26
100 Gunsmoke Street

The Ford County Government Center at the northwest corner of Central Avenue and Gunsmoke Street occupies the former Lora-Locke Hotel.

The Lora-Locke Hotel was constructed in 1928 as a 115-room luxury hostelry with a ballroom and restaurant. The five-story red brick structure, trimmed in Indiana limestone, was built by the Citizens' Hotel Company. The hotel was named to honor the wives of the owners. "Lora" was chosen for the wife of George S. Howell; "Locke" was the maiden name of Hattie Theis, the wife of Otto Theis.

The structure, designed by Ellis Charles and Company of Wichita, Kansas, and constructed by Eastergard and Bullard of McCook, Nebraska, was proclaimed a twentieth century marvel. The building was designed in two cubes, with an open area between, to aid in ventilation and provide each of the hotel rooms with windows. The hotel closed in 1978 and reopened under new management in 1984. It was listed on the National Register of Historic Places in 1985.

Facing overcrowding at the courthouse and with an opportunity to preserve a historical building, Ford County purchased the aging hotel in 1988. The structure was renovated and began a new chapter as the Ford County Government Center in 1991.

Fort Dodge Military Reservation Corner

Fort Dodge was established as a military post on the Santa Fe Trail in 1865. The military reservation included a 30,000-acre tract that was once part of the Osage Reservation.

A corner of the military reservation was established in what is now downtown Dodge City. The concrete marker in the sidewalk at the east entrance to the Ford County Government Center at Central and Military Avenues was placed in 1929 replacing the original limestone marker.

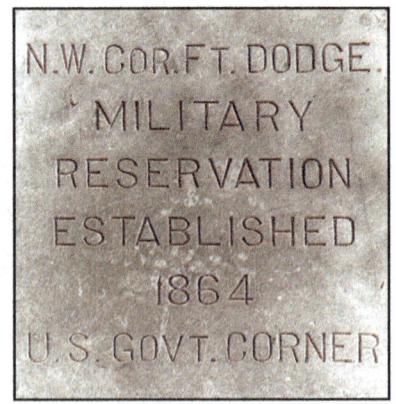

In 1880, portions of the military reservation were opened to settlement at $1.25 an acre. Fort Dodge was abandoned as a military post in 1882 and the soldiers were relocated at Camp Supply (Fort Supply, Oklahoma). In 1889, citizens of Dodge City purchased a 127-acre tract that included the fort and presented it to the State of Kansas for a soldiers' home.

The Kansas State Soldiers' Home, located five miles east of Dodge City on U.S. 400, has been in operation since 1890. Stone buildings constructed in 1867 continue to be utilized in the community. (see page 86)

Million Dollar Block
Howell Building, Dodge Theater   27
110 - 116 Gunsmoke Street

The Howell Building, constructed adjacent to the Lora-Locke Hotel in 1929, included a Montgomery Ward Store and the Dodge Theatre. The construction of this structure culminated a record setting building year in Dodge City that gave rise to the title "Million Dollar Block."

Other buildings contributing to the million dollar building-year included the First National Bank building, the International Harvester Plant, a five hundred thousand bushel grain elevator, the municipal building, an addition to Sacred Heart Catholic School, an apartment building and 100 homes. The million dollar figure was determined by amounts specified on the building permits. [30]

The Howell Building was constructed in the ornate Italian Renaissance style by Eastergard and Bullard of McCook, Nebraska. The facade is distinguished by quoined corners and arched windows with terracotta detailing in the arches above the upper windows.

The Dodge Theatre opened on October 18, 1929, featuring *The Love Doctor* starring Richard Dix and June Collyer. On April 1, 1939, the Dodge Theatre hosted the world premier of the Warner Brothers movie *Dodge City*. The demand for tickets was so great, however, that the premier was actually shown simultaneously at Dodge City's three theaters, all located within three blocks. More than fifty thousand people flocked to town for the gala festivities. The Hollywood entourage, arriving aboard the fourteen-car Warner Brothers Special, included cast members, additional Hollywood stars, Warner Brothers executives, and a newsreel crew. [31] (see page 43)

Chalk Beeson Theater   28
119 Gunsmoke Street

1930

1980

The name Beeson was synonymous with entertainment in the early days of Dodge City. Chalkley "Chalk" Beeson became the proprietor of Dodge City's Long Branch Saloon in 1876. He organized the nationally known Dodge City Cowboy Band shortly thereafter.

Merritt and Otie Beeson constructed this theater as a memorial to their father in 1915. Leading theatrical troupes and vaudeville acts traveling between Kansas City and Denver stopped in Dodge City to perform in the playhouse. With the advent of silent films and "talkies," the theater was converted into a motion picture theater.

In 1935, the theater was renovated into commercial space. An entrance on the west side of the building at 506 First Avenue led upstairs to a dance hall known as The Ritz. The USO was located at The Ritz from 1943 to 1945. A band made up of men stationed at the Dodge City Air Field provided the musical entertainment.

Dodge City Cowboy Band

Chalk Beeson led an effort to organize a community band in 1878. The band included musicians from the town's theaters and dance halls and was known as "Band of the Land" and later "Stockmen's Band." By 1881, the band was referred to as the Dodge City Cowboy Band.

The band played locally in front of the Long Branch Saloon on Front Street. Between 1884 and 1888, the band performed at stockmen's conventions in St. Louis, Kansas City and Denver.

At President Benjamin Harrison's inaugural celebration on March 4, 1889, the Cowboy Band lead the parade down Pennsylvania Avenue in Washington, D.C. Out in front of the band was the well-known frontiersman Buffalo Bill Cody.

After the engagement in Washington, the musicians disbanded. Beeson sold the charter and the band's regalia to Jack Sinclair in Idaho Springs, Colorado.

The Cowboy Band was reorganized in 1930 following state legislation allowing communities to support municipal bands through a mill levy. The Dodge City Municipal Cowboy Band, comprised of talented local musicians, performs a summer concert series at the Wright Park Bandshell on Tuesday evenings in June and July. The Cowboy Band also performs in the Dodge City Days Parade in the summer and hosts a Christmas concert.

Eisenhower Park, Murals   29
First Avenue and Gunsmoke Street

In 1989, vacant lots at the southwest corner of First Avenue and Gunsmoke Street were labeled an eyesore. This circumstance, however, provided an ideal location for a pocket-park in the downtown area. Betty Muncy, former publisher of the *Dodge City Daily Globe,* donated the lots to the City of Dodge City. The park was dedicated on July 21, 1990 during President Dwight Eisenhower's (1890 - 1969) centennial year. Eisenhower Park, with its covered stage, is a popular event site for downtown activities. The murals, described below, were painted by Inga Ojala, a Bucklin, Kansas artist, in 2022.

Dodge City Army Air Field, Dwight Eisenhower portrait

General Dwight Eisenhower, raised in Abilene, Kansas, served as Supreme Commander of the Allied forces during World War II. From 1942 to 1945, student officers, French nationals and Women's Air Force Service Pilots (WASPs) took flight instruction six miles northwest of town at the Dodge City Army Air Field. (see page 81)

J.C. Denious and Betty Muncy portrait

Jess Denious (1879 - 1953), was editor/publisher of the *Dodge City Daily Globe* from 1910 to 1953. He was president of the Dodge City Chamber of Commerce in 1942 when he lobbied the U.S. Government to locate the Army Airfield in Dodge City. Denious served as a state senator from 1932 to 1941 and as lieutenant governor during the administration of Governor Andrew Schoeppel (1943-1947). Martha Elizabeth "Betty" Muncy, Denious's daughter, was the publisher of the *Dodge City Daily Globe* from 1973 to 1988. She was a staunch supporter of the arts, a community volunteer and philanthropist. She was instrumental in raising funds for the restoration of the Santa Fe Depot for the Depot Theater Company.[32]

Cast of the 1939 Movie *Dodge City*

The premiere of the Warner Brothers film *Dodge City* was shown in the community on April 1, 1939. Hollywood movie stars attending the premiere traveled to town aboard a fourteen-car train dubbed the Warner Brothers Special. Cast members making the trip were: Errol Flynn, Ann Sheridan, and Alan Hale, Sr., Bruce Cabot, Frank McHugh and Guinn "Big Boy" Williams. Additional Hollywood stars attending were: Humphrey Bogart, Caire Windsor, John Garfield, Jane Wyman, Gilbert Roland, Mary Bryan, Wayne Morris, Marie Wilson, Maxie Rosenbloom, Gloria Dickson, Allan Jones, Lya Lys, John Payne, Jean Parker, Buck Jones, Frances Robinson, Hoot Gibson and the Lane sisters: Priscilla, Rosemary and Lola.[33] Co-star Olivia de Havilland did not attend the premiere due to the filming of *Gone With the Wind*.

Mexican Village, Louie Sanchez portrait

The Mexican Village mural is a tribute to the Dodge City colony of Mexican immigrants who were recruited as laborers by the Atchison, Topeka and Santa Fe Railroad. The Village was located east of the Santa Fe Depot on five and a half acres in the rail yard. The community had a grocery store, a school and a Catholic church. The dancing *senorita* serves as a reminder that community hosted annual fiestas, first in the Village and later in Wright Park, from the 1920s

to the 1950s. The portrait of Louis Sanchez (1923-2020), honors the first Hispanic mayor of Dodge City, who was born and raised in the Village. The five flags in the mural identify the of countries of Spain, France, Mexico, the Republic of Texas, and the United States, that have flown over Dodge City.

First School Site   30
208 Gunsmoke Street

The first school in Dodge City was a one-room frame structure located on the northwest corner of First Avenue and Walnut (now Gunsmoke) Street. Margaret Walker taught the original class of eleven students. The building was used as a primary school from 1873 until 1880 when it was abandoned for a newly-constructed brick building on Boot Hill.

In 1913, the frame building was razed in advance of a growing business district. Southwest Bell Telephone Company commemorated the site in 1927 with a plaque affixed to a large bell-shaped granite stone. The plaque was later attached to the telephone building.

St. Cornelius Episcopal Church   31
200 West Spruce Street

St. Cornelius Church is the oldest house of worship still in use in Dodge City. The church was constructed in 1898 from sandstone originally used in an ice house.

The structure was designed by William B. Kimball of Milwaukee, Wisconsin; the builder was A.B. Metcalfe of Dodge City. The architecture is a mixture of Norman and Gothic styles. A castle tower and Gothic archway compose the main entrance.

On May 2, 1888, the Episcopal mission was organized in Dodge City. The church was built under the direction of Rev. Dr. D.J. Krum, rector of the church and general missionary for

southwest Kansas. The Rt. Rev. Frank R. Millspaugh, bishop of Kansas, consecrated the church on September 11, 1898.

The name St. Cornelius was chosen for the Episcopal mission because of Dodge City's close association with Fort Dodge. St. Cornelius was a Roman solider and the captain of one hundred men. He became one of the first Gentile converts and later the first bishop of Caesarea. It is believed that this church is the only Episcopal mission in the United States named for St. Cornelius.

Gospel Hill

The location of Union Church came by its moniker, Gospel Hill, naturally. The community's frontier house of worship stood on the northeast corner of First Avenue and Spruce Street, atop a hill directly opposite of Boot Hill Cemetery. The church-goers departing after services had a plain view of the cemetery to the west and notorious Front Street to the south.

The Union Church, constructed in 1876, was a community church. Itinerant ministers conducted services irregularly. As the population increased, denominations were organized.

Gospel Hill expanded in scope as congregations constructed separate churches. The Presbyterians (1878), the Catholics (1882), the Methodists (1884), the Baptists (1885), the Christian congregation (1886), and the Episcopalians (1898) all constructed churches in the vicinity of Gospel Hill.[34]

Law Enforcement Officers Memorial   32
110 West Spruce Street

A monument outside the Dodge City Police Department honors Dodge City lawmen who lost their lives in the line of duty:

City Marshal Edward J. Masterson - April 9, 1878: Killed attempting to disarm drunken cowboy, Jack Wagner, who also died as a result of the gun battle.[35]

Assistant City Marshal Tom Nixon - July 21, 1884: Shot and killed by Dave Mather over an old grudge.[36]

Chief of Police J.E. Cox - November 8, 1927: Killed in a shootout with John Waychoff, a suspected chicken thief, who himself was killed the following morning in a gunfight with officers twenty miles southwest of Garden City, Kansas.[37]

Police Officer LeRoy Davis - May, 18, 1929: Shot and killed by Roy Redding, suspected auto thief. Redding was apprehended the following day near Holcomb, Kansas. He was charged with murder, pleaded guilty, and sentenced to life in prison.[38]

Ford County Courthouse   33
101 West Spruce Street

Ford County was among a group of counties created by the Kansas Legislature in 1867. It was named in honor of Colonel James H. Ford, who is credited with the establishment of Fort Dodge. [39]

The county's first courthouse was constructed on this site of brick and native stone in 1876. The present courthouse was constructed between 1912 and 1913. The architect was Reuel A. Curtis of Kansas City, Missouri; the builder was George Shaul of Seneca, Kansas.

The structure was designed in the Neo-Classical style. Both the Doric columns and pediments at the entrances were common in the design of Greek temples. The Bedford limestone exterior and Berea limestone columns add a classical grace to the building.

In 1993, the interior of the courthouse was completely renovated as a district court building; the county offices moved to the Ford County Government Center (see page 38). The architect was Gossen, Livingston and Associates of Wichita; the builder was Rhodes Construction of Dodge City.

U.S. Post Office   34
700 Central Avenue

Dodge City's federal building was constructed between 1931 and 1932. The structure was designed by James W. Wetmore in Italian Renaissance style. A clay-tile roof surmounts the building; buff-colored pilasters with Corinthian capitals flank the main entrance; colorful terracotta enhances the archways around the widows.

Mail service in the area began two miles west of the future Dodge City at Fort Atkinson. [40] Later a post office was established at Fort Dodge on October 24, 1865. Service was discontinued and re-established twice at the fort. The present postal service was established at Fort Dodge on April 29, 1872, and transferred to Dodge City on September 23, 1872. [41]

The federal building housed the weather bureau from 1932 to 1942, before it relocated to the Dodge City Municipal Airport. The weather bureau was first established in Dodge City on September 15, 1874, and was located in a number of buildings. Prior to the construction of the federal building, the weather bureau occupied a frame building on this same site from 1909 to 1931. During the construction of the federal building, the weather bureau was temporarily located in the First National Bank building.

Old Ford County Health Department Building   35
106 East Spruce

This one and a half-story concrete building was constructed for the Ford County Welfare Department by the Works Progress Administration (WPA) in 1938. The vertical and bands on the facade are representative of Art Deco design.

During the Depression, the county relief building was the local center for agencies created through President Franklin Roosevelt's New Deal program. The first floor housed offices for the Agricultural Adjustment Administration (AAA), the Farm Security Administration's soil conservation engineers, and case workers in the relief department.

The basement served as a warehouse for commodity distribution for twenty-four counties in southwest Kansas. The basement was also utilized as a sewing room where WPA workers made garments for the disadvantaged. During World War II, the sewing room was used by Red Cross volunteers to complete unfinished garments and surgical dressings.

The Ford County Health Department utilized the building for forty years before moving to a new facility at 507 Avenue L in 2017.

Home of Stone   36
112 East Vine Street

The Home of Stone, also known as the Mueller-Schmidt House, was constructed between 1879 and 1881 and is one of the oldest homes in Dodge City.

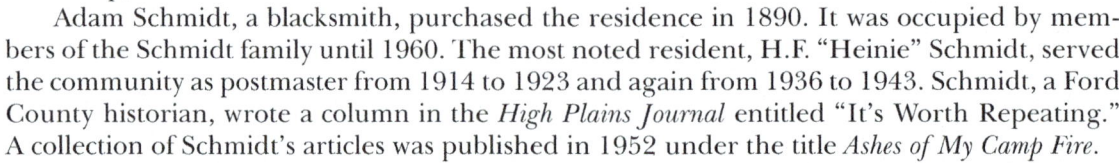

William Hessman, a stone mason originally from Germany, together with his sons, constructed the residence of limestone cut and faced at a quarry on Sawlog Creek, twelve miles northeast of Dodge City. The stones were cut two feet thick and set with limestone mortar described as being hard as steel.

John Mueller, a boot-maker and cattle rancher, was the original owner. After a blizzard in 1886 devastated his cattle investment and a fire on Front Street destroyed his boot shop, Mueller sold out and moved to St. Louis.

Adam Schmidt, a blacksmith, purchased the residence in 1890. It was occupied by members of the Schmidt family until 1960. The most noted resident, H.F. "Heinie" Schmidt, served the community as postmaster from 1914 to 1923 and again from 1936 to 1943. Schmidt, a Ford County historian, wrote a column in the *High Plains Journal* entitled "It's Worth Repeating." A collection of Schmidt's articles was published in 1952 under the title *Ashes of My Camp Fire*.

The Home of Stone was purchased by Ford County in 1965 and is now operated as a museum by the Ford County Historical Society. Named to the National Register of Historic Places in 1972, the Home of Stone features a hand-carved walnut spiral staircase and Victorian-era furnishings.

Bat Masterson Statue

William Barclay "Bat" Masterson, who served the community as Ford County Sheriff from 1877 to 1879 and later as a member of the Dodge City Peace Commission, is memorialized in a bronze sculpture outside the Home of Stone. Norton Enterprises of Leoti, Kansas, was commissioned by the Ford County Historical Society to create the sculpture. The artists depicted Masterson fittingly for his nickname "the Dandy." He is "dressed to the nines, with a little bit of swagger" leaning on a saloon bar in derby hat and suit with his iconic cane. The sculpture was dedicated June 19, 2022. [42]

Masterson was a buffalo hunter, gunfighter, lawman, and gambler. He moved to Colorado in the mid-1880s and in 1902 left for New York City where he worked for *The Morning Telegraph* as a reporter and columnist. Masterson wrote about sports, particularly boxing, crime, war and politics. He died at his desk from a heart attack on October 21, 1921. He is buried at Woodlawn Cemetery in the Bronx.

Presbyterian Church 37
803 Central Avenue

In 1877, Rev. Ormond W. Wright preached at the newly constructed Union Church. The following year he organized the Presbyterian Church in Dodge City. The congregation constructed its own church on Central Avenue in 1880.

In 1909, an addition was constructed to accommodate a pipe organ. That structure served the congregation until 1924 when work was initiated on a stone church. During construction, the congregation met in the Ford County Courthouse.

The Gothic stone church was built under the direction of Rev. George F. McDougall. It was designed by Harry W. Jones of Minneapolis, Minnesota; the builders were J.N. Parham of Dodge City and Hatfield Construction of Kinsley, Kansas. The church was dedicated on September 27, 1925.

The Church Bell Setting

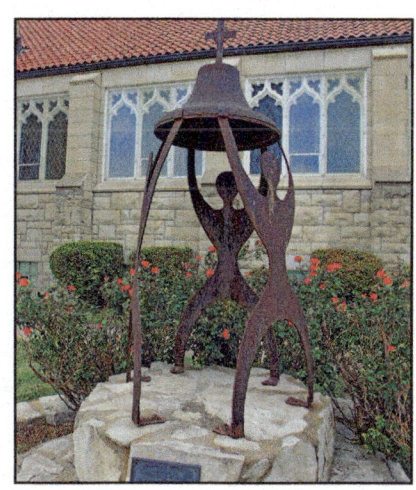

To commemorate the Presbyterian congregation's 100th anniversary, a sculpture was commissioned in 1978. The artwork was designed by architect G.L. Weaver and sculpted by Lowell Tasset, both of Dodge City. The sculpture includes the bell from the first church upheld by three figures, symbolizing the unified effort of many persons carrying on the work of the church.

The bell was originally a gift from Rev. Wright's home church in Ripley, New York. The church bell setting was dedicated to the memory of the Clarence Nevins and Thomas Gray families, faithful supporters of the Presbyterian Church.

Hinkle-Heinz House 38
801 First Avenue

The Hinkle-Heinz House is a small wood-frame home constructed in 1880. It is one of the oldest residences in Dodge City and represents a middle-income home from the late nineteenth century. The original floor plan included a parlor, kitchen and bedroom. The covered porch was a common feature of the era. The home is a designated city landmark, listed on the Register of Historic Kansas Places, and a contributing property in the National Register Historic District. [43]

George Hinkle was a bartender on Front Street at George Hoover's Wholesale Liquors and Saloon. He defeated Bat Masterson in an election for Ford County Sheriff and served from 1880 to 1884. Hinkle sold the home to Charles Heinz, the owner of the Lone Star Saloon, in 1883. A number of families lived in the residence, but eventually the property was abandoned and the home was slated to be torn down. Local historians rallied to save the home and volunteer groups renovated the property through Interfaith Housing Services. The home is occupied as a private residence. [44]

Sughrue Home 39
810 Central Avenue

The Sughrue name is well-known for the many peace officers in the family. P.H. Sughrue came to Dodge City in 1885 to visit his cousins, the famous twin sheriffs, Pat and Mike Sughrue. Pat Sughrue served Ford County as sheriff from 1884 to 1887; Mike Sughrue served Clark County as sheriff from 1885 to 1901. P.H. Sughrue stayed in Dodge City and was the town marshal between 1891 and 1893. Pat's son, Joe, the model for the Cowboy Statue on Boot Hill, was assistant marshal in 1920 and marshal from 1933 to 1936. John Sughrue, a son of P.H., was deputy sheriff and a policeman during the 1930s and 1940s.

P.H. Sughrue purchased this house in 1915. For the next sixty-three years, members of the Sughrue family resided in the home. Herbert Sughrue, John's son, and his wife Kath-

ryn, were the last members of the family to live in the home. Kathryn was elected to the Kansas House of Representatives from the 116th District in 1976 and served fourteen years.

The most significant features of this Colonial Revival villa are the Palladian windows in the gables and the columned porch. Originally the third floor of the house was built as a billiards room. The living room was designed after the Hamilton Room in the White House. Decorative ironwork enhances the patio and garden areas. The home, designated city landmark, remains a private residence.

Sacred Heart Cathedral   40
903 Central Avenue

Sacred Heart Cathedral was constructed between 1915 and 1916. The church was designed by Cram and Ferguson of Boston, Massachusetts; the builder was W.B. Foley of Dodge City.

The church, built under the direction of Father John M. Handly, is designed in the Spanish Renaissance style. The off-center bell tower, stucco finish and red-tile roof are characteristic of a Spanish Mission. The ornate carving around the doorway is reminiscent of the Baroque architecture of eighteenth century Spain. Two tiers of stained glass windows, created by Emil Frei Studios of St. Louis, feature images of the Twelve Apostles and missionary saints.

The church was dedicated on August 4, 1916. It replaced a frame church constructed on this site in 1882. Sacred Heart Church became a cathedral when the Catholic Diocese of Dodge City was established in 1952. Sacred Heart Cathedral was placed on the National Register of Historic Places in 1982, the centennial year of the parish.

Since the Cathedral of Our Lady of Guadalupe was constructed in 2001 at 2341 North 14th Street, the church has been utilized for Masses for the students at Sacred Heart School, and some funerals and weddings.

Crucifixion on Calvary

The Crucifixion of Jesus Christ is depicted in a twenty-six foot square, oil on canvas mural behind the altar in Sacred Heart Cathedral. The mural was painted in 1916 by George Melville Stone of Topeka, Kansas.

This Crucifixion scene is unique. The character in the left foreground has the facial features of a Native American; the flora is that of the prairie and the centurion's horse is a pinto pony. The mural was painted in this fashion at the request of Father Handly.

Only one model was used for the painting. Sister Agnes Curran, C.S.J., a teacher at St. Mary of the Plains Academy, was viewing the unfinished work and the artist asked to sketch her profile for the Blessed Virgin Mary.

Our Lady of the Plains

A second oil on canvas mural is located in back of the church. *Our Lady of the Plains* was originally the altar mural in the sanctuary of the chapel at St. Mary of the Plains College (SMPC). The mural was painted by Milton Frenzel of Emil Frei Studios, St. Louis, Missouri, in 1952. After the college closed in 1992, the canvas was removed from the chapel wall and installed at Sacred Heart Cathedral.

The painting depicts the Blessed Virgin Mary, the patroness of the college, dressed in robes of blue and white. At the sides of the Virgin Mary are a meadowlark and a sunflower, Kansas state symbols. The evolution of the Kansas plains is shown in the foreground. Pictured are a herd of buffalo, an Indian, the Spanish explorer Francisco Vasquez de Coronado, the conquistador Espejo, Franciscan Friar Juan de Padilla, a cowboy and farm family, kneeling in a wheat field with an oil derrick nearby. This compilation is surmounted by the St. Mary of the Plains Academy building, the predecessor, of the college.

District Two

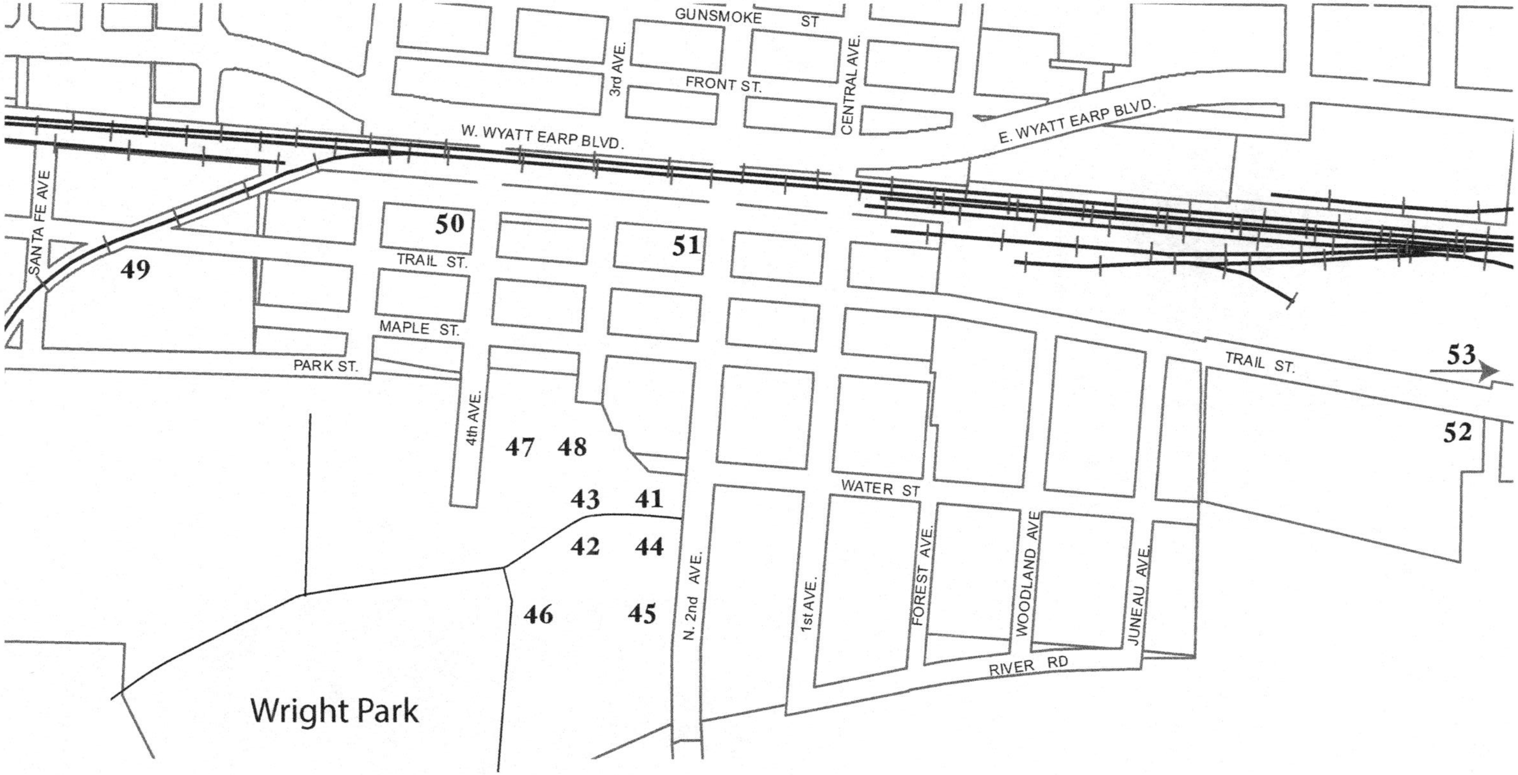

Wright Park

41. Wright Park
42. Wright – Mootz Memorial
43. Santa Fe Trail Marker
44. Mill Wheel
45. Lone Tree, Riney Bridge Markers
46. Municipal Bandshell
47. Hoover Pavilion

48. Liberty Garden
49. Kansas Power Company Plant
50. Guymon Petro Mercantile Building
51. Sod House Site
52. Mexico Border Marker
53. Panoramic Mural

Wright Park   41
71 N. Second Ave.

Wright Park memorializes the name of Robert M. Wright, a director of the Dodge City Town Company, early-day businessman and civic leader.

Wright was born in Bladensburg, Maryland, in 1840. He traveled West at the age of sixteen and lived on a farm near St. Louis until 1859. During the next eight years, he worked as a trader and contractor, hauling grain and cutting hay and wood for military posts along the Santa Fe Trail.

In 1867, Wright became co-owner of the sutler store at Fort Dodge. One month prior to the organization of the town company in 1872, Wright joined in partnership with Charles Rath and A.J. Anthony to establish a headquarters for the sale of general merchandise on the future Dodge City town site.

Charles Rath and Company initially was the outfitter for buffalo hunters. The firm operated a hide yard on the grounds of the Santa Fe Depot. It was not uncommon to see 40,000 hides stacked in the rail yard awaiting shipment to the East. Between 1872 and 1874, over 850,000 buffalo hides were shipped from Dodge City.

In 1876, Rath sold out to Wright who took in Henry Beverley as a partner. The Wright Beverly Company distributed merchandise over hundreds of miles of territory. Cattlemen and drovers replaced the buffalo hunters when Dodge City became the Kansas railhead for the Texas cattle drives. After driving the Longhorn herds to town, the drovers could buy almost anything they desired from the store's inventory valued at $40,000.

In 1883, Wright purchased nearly twenty acres of treeless swampland north of the Arkansas River from the Dodge City Town Company. The parcel included several small channels of the river. In the legal description, the south boundary of the property was defined by the north bank of Arkansas River and its meanderings.

Wright intended to give the city the land as a park. In order to prevent erosion during spring flooding, he closed the channels with levees. With the channels closed, the main stream of the river meandered southward. Accretions from the meandering river expanded the south boundary of the property. In 1900, the parcel of land was deeded to the City of Dodge City and the park was named in Wright's honor.

Wright Park has expanded to include property to the west. The sixty-one acre park includes the Dodge City Zoo, the Hoover Pavilion, a bandshell, the Long Branch Lagoon water park, KOA RV park and cabins, a skateboard park, dog park, shelter houses and soccer fields. The grounds are enhanced with large shade trees surrounding memorials and monuments of historical significance.

Robert M. Wright served Dodge City as mayor from 1885 to 1886 and represented Ford County in the Kansas Legislature from 1875 to 1883. Throughout his life, "Bob" Wright worked to benefit the community. He was considered by some to be "Mr. Dodge City."

Robert Wright, who was Kansas Commissioner of Forestry from 1899 to 1903, designed the park and engaged Peter Mootz, a local nursery man, with the landscaping. Mootz, together with the help of transient workers, transported cottonwood saplings by horse-drawn wagon from the banks of the Sawlog Creek in northern Ford County. The fast-growing cottonwoods kept the soil from eroding and provided shade and shape to the land.

A monument to honor Wright and Mootz was originally the idea of a man named Pierce Hobble, a railroad fireman. In 1913 a limestone column was broken during the construction of the Ford County Courthouse. Hobble obtained the lower portion of the column to erect a monument in the park.

This well-intending citizen was persuaded to give up the idea of creating the monument by himself by those who believed that it should be a community project. The broken column lay idle in the park until 1934, when Works Progress Administration workers constructing the bandshell set it on a stone foundation. The monument was not completed until 1952 when a bronze plaque

was placed on the column acknowledging its purpose. In 1971, the plaque was stolen, leaving the monument void of a marker until 1980, when an aluminum reproduction was cast.

Santa Fe Trail Marker   43

Some 500 miles of the 775-mile Santa Fe Trail between Independence, Missouri and Santa Fe, snaked through Kansas. In 1906, the Kansas Chapter of the Daughters of the American Revolution (DAR) placed red granite markers along the roadways at points where highways either follow or cross the original routes of the trail. [45]

From Fort Dodge, through what is now Dodge City, the trail followed the north bank of the Arkansas River before reaching the Cimarron Crossing. This marker was originally located at the northwest corner of Second Avenue and Trail Street. Road construction in 1980 necessitated its relocation to Wright Park.

Mill Wheel   44

This mill wheel stands as a monument to the area wheat and flour industry. It was placed in Wright Park in 1978 through the efforts of the Ford County Historical Society and Cal Trent, a former Dodge City Mill Flour employee.

The six-ton wheel was a replacement wheel stored at the Dodge City Flour Mill. The mill, located on the northeast corner of Second Avenue and Trail Street, was constructed between 1907 and 1908. It was purchased by the Colorado Milling Company in 1918. That company continued operating the mill until April 4, 1949, when it was destroyed by fire.

After the fire, the original mill wheel was sold as scrap metal. When in use, the wheel was pulled by a 450-horsepower motor with a ninety-six-foot leather strap. The mill wheel was an essential element in the machinery that produced an average of 1,400 two hundred-pound barrels of flour every twenty-four hours.

The Lone Sentinel, named by the Kiowa Indians, was a giant cottonwood tree that stood just north of the Arkansas River along what is today Second Avenue. The tree marked an area where the river could be forded.

In the early days of Dodge City, the tree was used as a billboard and for target practice. Tradition has it that several horse thieves were hanged from the tree.

And then there is the story regarding vaudeville actor Eddie Foy, who in the summer of 1878, performed at Theatre Comique

Circa 1934

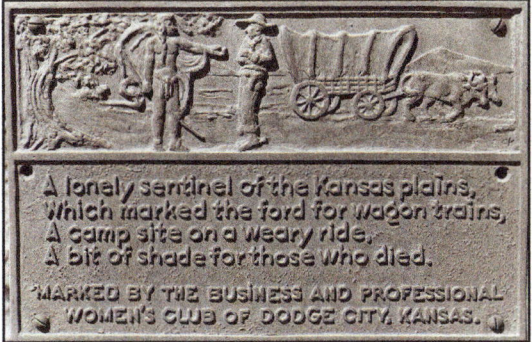

on Front Street. A group of rowdy cowboys marched Foy down to the tree and threatened to hang him. The "joke" ended with Foy buying a round of drinks at the nearest saloon.[46] Undeterred, he returned to perform at the theatre the following summer.

The Business and Professional Women's Club placed a plaque on the tree in 1929. The poem on the plaque was written by Lester Schoof, an assistant postmaster and a local historian. The cottonwood stood as sentinel over the river for more than a century. It lived to see three bridges span the river.

Shortly after the third bridge was constructed in 1935, the tree died. It remained standing until 1938 when decay forced it to topple. The plaque, formerly attached to the tree, is now included in a setting with the Riney Bridge plaque east of a shelter house near Second Avenue.

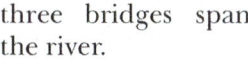

1887

RINEY BRIDGE

DEDICATED TO
THE MEMORY
OF
JOHN T RINEY

PIONEER, TOWN LEADER,
RAILROAD BUILDER, STOCKMAN,
WAGON FREIGHTER, DAIRYMAN

ON THIS SITE HE BUILT AND OPERATED
A TOLL BRIDGE OVER WHICH PASSED
SETTLERS' WAGONS TO THE SOUTHWEST,
WAGON FREIGHTERS TO FORT SUPPLY,
AND TEXAS CATTLE HERDS TO THE
RAILHEAD AT DODGE CITY.

Riney Bridge

In 1873, a group of prominent businessmen organized the Dodge City Bridge Company. That same year, a toll bridge was constructed of oak planks shipped by rail from Fort Madden, Iowa. John T. Riney was hired to collect tolls. The concrete bridge, now spanning the Arkansas River at Second Avenue memorializes his name.

The wooden bridge, the first to cross the river in all of western Kansas, was considered the gateway to the southwest. When high waters prohibited fording the stream, the bridge was the only way to cross the once turbulent river.

Riney, who lived on the north bank in a small house, collected one dollar for a wagon pulled by a two-horse team; $2.50 for a freight wagon pulled by a team of six or eight; twenty-five cents for a saddle horse, and ten cents for a pedestrian.

Riney continued as tollkeeper until 1885. On July 3, 1885, a county-wide referendum on bridge bonds passed. The Ford County Commissioners purchased the bridge for $6,000, assuring free passage over the river for everyone.

In 1906, the wooden bridge was replaced with a steel bridge. In 1935, a four-lane concrete bridge replaced the steel bridge. It wasn't until 1967 that it was discovered that the Kansas Department of Transportation had officially named the structure Riney Bridge.

Circa 1906

Through the efforts of the Ford County Historical Society, a rededication ceremony was held and a plaque honoring Riney was placed on the northwest bridge railing. That plaque is now part of the aforementioned park setting.

Municipal Bandshell   46

The bandshell was constructed by Civil Works Administration laborers under the direction of W.D. Orebaugh of Dodge City. The building plan was designed by Carl Mershon, Dodge City architect. The unusual bandshell is a frame truncated cone of five concentric circles with stucco finish. The base and speaker towers are constructed of native stone. The bandshell, constructed at a cost of $4,000, was dedicated with a Fourth of July concert in 1934. It is used for a variety of summertime activities, in particular, concerts performed by the Dodge City Cowboy Band on Tuesday evenings in June and July.

Hoover Pavilion   47

This public meeting hall is a memorial pavilion named for Dodge City's first elected mayor, George M. Hoover. Few citizens have contributed as much to the community as Hoover. At the time of his death, July 14, 1914, Hoover left $100,000 of an estate valued at $250,000 for the upkeep and beautification of city property. The pavilion was constructed in 1919 with $10,000 earmarked in Hoover's will for a public meeting hall.

An addition was constructed in 1939 as an armory for the local Kansas National Guard unit. The architectural firm was Mann and Gerow of Hutchinson; the builder was J.N. Parham of Dodge City. In 1959, the National Guard unit moved to a new armory constructed at Central Avenue and Soule Street.

The Spanish-styled pavilion is dressed in stucco and surmounted by a red-title roof. Originally the archways were open. This aided ventilation in the summer months but prevented heating in the winter. In 1952, the pavilion was transformed when the archways were redesigned as windows and doors.

George M. Hoover inadvertently had something to do with the location of Dodge City. In 1872, Colonel Richard Irving Dodge, the commander at Fort Dodge, prohibited the sale of liquor on the military reservation. The boundary of the reservation extend five miles west of the fort.

On June 17, 1872, Hoover tied a rag to a wheel of his wagon loaded with whiskey and headed west. After he had measured off five miles, Hoover opened a make-shift saloon on a foot-wide board supported by stacked sod. From tent saloon keeper, Hoover became a prominent businessman with a wholesale liquor establishment on Front Street.

The Hoover Fund, established as an endowment, is still utilized by the City of Dodge City for beautification projects. [47]

Liberty Garden   48

On September 11, 2001, nineteen al Qaeda terrorists hijacked four commercial airliners in a strategically planned attack against the United States. Two of the airliners crashed into the Twin Towers at the World Trade Center in New York City. One airliner crashed into the Pentagon in Arlington, Virginia. The fourth airliner, destined for the United States Capitol in Washington, D.C., crashed into a field near Shanksville, Pennsylvania. The terrorists crashed into the field rather than have passengers and crew regain control of the aircraft. [48]

Nearly 3,000 people were killed in the attacks. 412 emergency workers and 343 firefighters lost their lives. Six thousand people were injured, many of whom survived thanks to the first responders. [49]

On the first anniversary of the terrorist attack, September 11, 2002, the Liberty Garden in Wright Park was dedicated as Dodge City's 911 Memorial. The memorial includes two reflective pools with stainless steel likenesses of the Twin Towers. Between the reflective pools at each end are pieces of structural steel from the Twin Towers; limestone from the Pentagon, and a stone from the Pennsylvania crash site.

The 911 memorial was designed by the Liberty Garden Committee and the Dodge City Puddles and Pads Pond Club. The concept of creating Liberty Gardens across the United States originated with Keep America Beautiful, a national advocate for community beautification. As an affiliate of Keep America Beautiful, the City of Dodge City was made aware that structural steel from the Twin Towers could be requested. The committee then made the appropriate contacts for items from the two other crash sites.

The Liberty Garden is the site of Dodge City's annual September 11 Day of Remembrance Service. The community, together with law enforcement, firefighters, and first responders, pause to remember those who lost their lives in the terrorist attack and the servicemen and women who continue to serve in the fight against terrorism.

Kansas Power Company Plant   49
709 West Trail Street

The first utility franchise was awarded to the Dodge City Incandescent Electric Light Company in 1886. On August 21, 1886, electric lights illuminated Dodge City's nights.

The franchise became the Dodge City Electric Light and Steam Heating Company in 1887. During that same year, the downtown area was equipped with street lights.

The building known as the Kansas Power Company Plant was constructed around 1907 and has housed a number of companies. [50] In 1911, the electric franchise was awarded to the Midland Water and Light and Ice Company. The Kansas Power Company occupied the plant from 1927 to 1969. Successive owners were: Central Telephone and Utilities Corporation, Centel Corporation and Utilicorp. By 1996, the original power plant was sold and no longer produced electricity. [51]

In 2016, the building, now occupied by Sgt. Pyle's Auto Repair, was listed on the Register of Historic Kansas Places for its association with the early history of Dodge City's public works and energy development. The buff-colored stucco building is accentuated with distinctive one and two story arched window bays surrounded by brick. The cornice atop the walls consists of built-up brick in an arched pattern capped with a brick parapet.

Guymon Petro Mercantile Building   50
301 Fourth Avenue

The Cowboy Capital Saloon and Grill, south of Boot Hill Museum, occupies a former wholesale food warehouse.

The two-story red brick structure was constructed in 1912 at a cost of $3,000 by the Dodge City Wholesale Grocery Company. The Guymon Petro Mercantile Company purchased the building in 1946 and continued operations at the site until 1957.

The first floor of the building sits on a raised concrete foundation for ease of loading and unloading goods from rail cars on the Rock Island tracks. Atop the structure is a stepped brick corbel parapet. The name of the mercantile company, after having faded over the years, was repainted in 2016.

The large bay window areas on the east side of the restaurant were originally loading docks for delivery trucks that provided dry goods and produce to thirty-six mom and pop neighborhood groceries in town. [52] Guymon Petro also supplied grocery stores outside of Dodge City and was known as the largest wholesale distributing firm in southwest Kansas.

Prior to becoming a bar and grill, the building was used as storage for the Boot Hill Museum. The structure was donated to Steve Olson who opened the restaurant in 2016. Later that same year, Olson purchased Bat Masterson's pocket watch at an auction and presented the historical artifact to the museum. Masterson received the watch at a Fourth of July celebration in 1885 after he was voted, "The most popular man in Dodge City." [53] (see page 48)

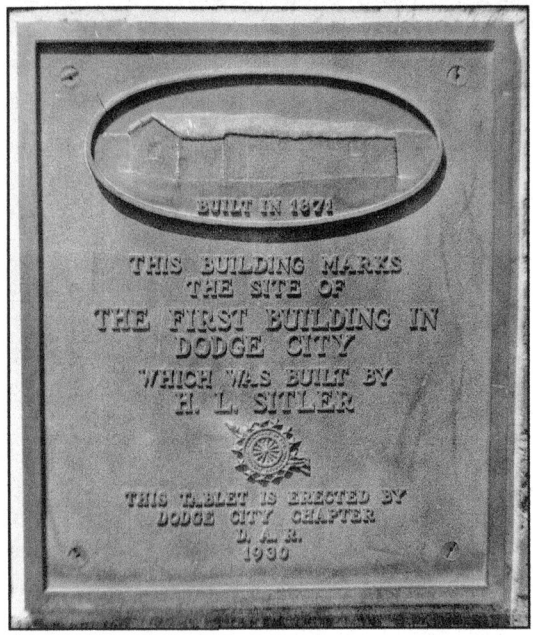

BUILT IN 1871

THIS BUILDING MARKS
THE SITE OF
THE FIRST BUILDING IN
DODGE CITY
WHICH WAS BUILT BY
H. L. SITLER

THIS TABLET IS ERECTED BY
DODGE CITY CHAPTER
D. A. R.
1930

Sod House Site   51
305 Second Avenue

The first structure in Dodge City was a three-room sod house constructed in 1871 prior to the town's establishment. Henry L. Sitler, who a year later became a director of the Dodge City Town Company, built the structure beside the Santa Fe Trail.

Sitler supplied hay and wood to military posts under a government contract. The sod house was his headquarters and an overnight stop between freighting between Fort Hays and Camp Supply (Fort Supply, Oklahoma).

A plaque commemorating the sod house site was placed on the building, now occupied by Lopp Motors, in 1940 by the Dodge City Chapter of the Daughters of the American Revolution.

Mexico Border Marker #30   52
503 East Trail Street

A metal obelisk outside the entrance to Casey's Cowtown Club is one of forty-seven markers placed along the 1819 border between Mexico and the United States during a project named DeLIMITations. In 2014, Marcos Ramirez, an artist who tackles border topics in sculptural works, and David Taylor, an Arizona photographer, set out on a 3,721-mile journey to mark the international boundary defined by the Treaty of Adams-Onis. [54] The markers extend from Brookings, Oregon, in the northwest, to Port Arthur, Texas. The marker in Dodge City sets a ninety degree corner between markers from the west at Syracuse, Kansas, and to the south at Englewood, Kansas.

Panoramic Mural   53
2000 East Trail Street

A short course in Dodge City's history from the late 1880s to the early 1900s is illustrated in a mural extending 270 feet across the front of the National Beef plant. The mural consists of historic scenes that include wildlife, early inhabitants, modes of transportation, lifestyles and industries.

The mural, originally painted by Stan Herd in 1985, included sixteen scenes. Due to weathering and fading, Herd repainted the mural on marine plywood in 2002. Several panels were later relocated due to plant expansion (see pages 23 and 37). In 2018, the mural panels were removed from the building and photographed. After the colors were digitally restored, the mural was printed on vinyl banner material that was stretched and installed into a mounted frame system. The iconic piece has now been preserved through technology for future reprints as the western Kansas elements eventually take their toll.

The original plant, Hyplains Dress Beef, was founded by Sam Davis in 1961. It was the first beef packing plant located at the source of live cattle in southwest Kansas. The plant processed 150 cattle a day, or 750 per week. By 1986, the facility was processing 11,400 cattle per week. The plant was purchased in 1991 and has been known as National Beef since that time. The expanded facility processes 6,000 cattle a day, or between 30,000 and 36,000 weekly depending on a five or six day work week. National Beef employs 3,000 people in Dodge City. Beef and beef by-products are shipped throughout the nation and to international markets.

District Three

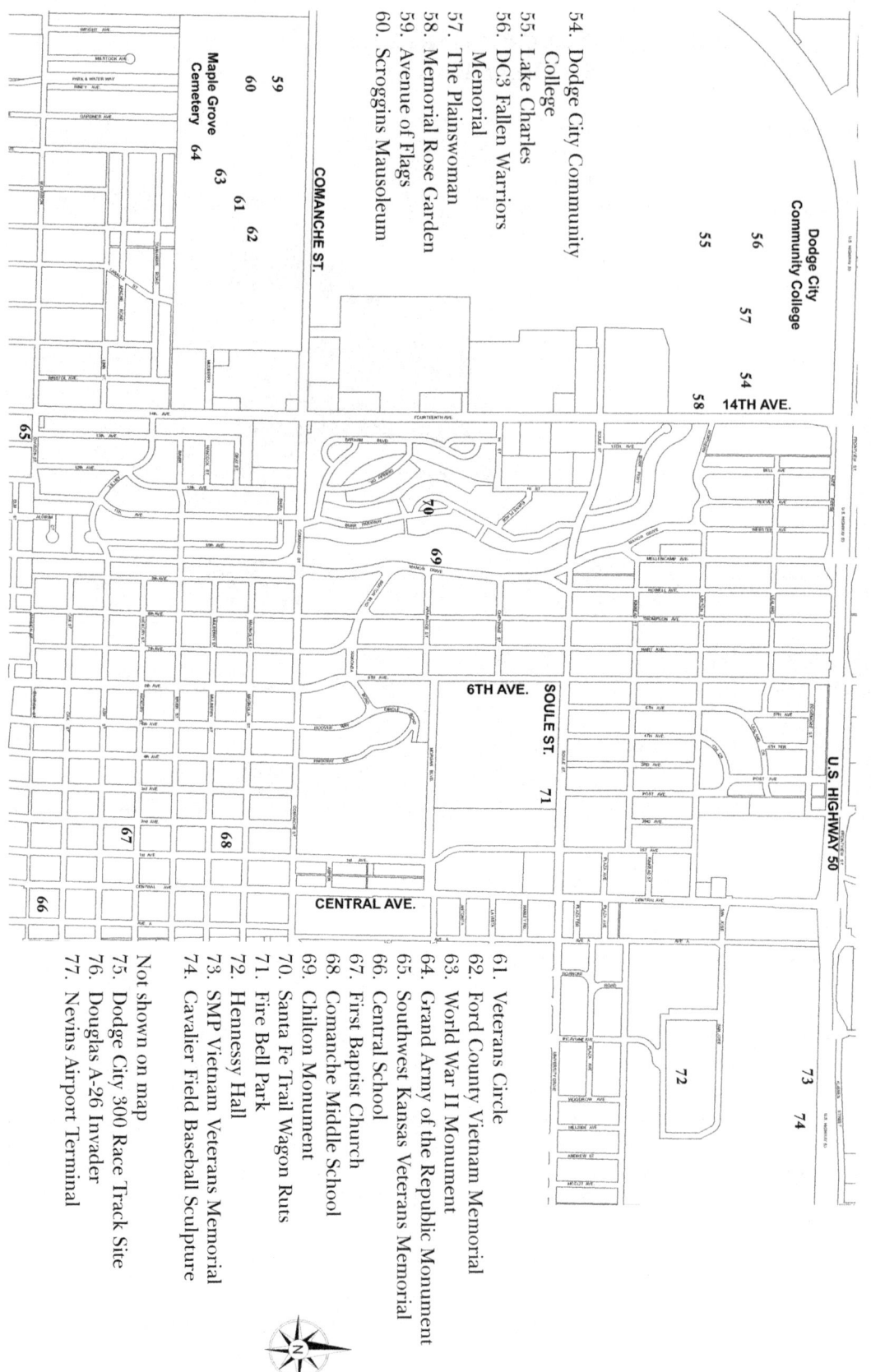

54. Dodge City Community College
55. Lake Charles
56. DC3 Fallen Warriors Memorial
57. The Plainswoman
58. Memorial Rose Garden
59. Avenue of Flags
60. Scroggins Mausoleum

61. Veterans Circle
62. Ford County Vietnam Memorial
63. World War II Monument
64. Grand Army of the Republic Monument
65. Southwest Kansas Veterans Memorial
66. Central School
67. First Baptist Church
68. Comanche Middle School
69. Chilton Monument
70. Santa Fe Trail Wagon Ruts
71. Fire Bell Park
72. Hennessy Hall
73. SMP Vietnam Veterans Memorial
74. Cavalier Field Baseball Sculpture

Not shown on map
75. Dodge City 300 Race Track Site
76. Douglas A-26 Invader
77. Nevins Airport Terminal

Dodge City Community College   54
2501 North 14th Avenue

Dodge City Community College has a history dating back to 1935. Previous names for the institution were Dodge City Junior College, Dodge City College, and Dodge City Community Junior College.

The college has operated at three locations: the third floor of the former Dodge City High School building at 1601 First Avenue from 1935 to 1957; the former Junior High School building at 1000 North Second Avenue from 1957 to 1970, and the current campus on 14th Avenue since 1970. [55]

The campus was dedicated on October 25, 1970. Caudill Rowlett Scott, a Houston-based architectural firm, designed the campus. The affiliate architectural firm was Gurtner and Robison of Dodge City. Johnson Builders of Salina was the contractor. Caudill Rowlett Scott was recognized for its design work with an Honor Award from the Texas Society of Architects in 1971.

Lake Charles 55

The namesake for Lake Charles is Dr. Charles Barnes who served twenty-three consecutive years as the chief administrator of the college, first as dean (1959 to 1965), and then as president (1965 to 1982).

When Dr. Barnes became dean of the college in 1959, the institution was governed by the local school district. He worked with State Senator Laurin Jones to create a community college system funded on a county-wide basis independent of local school boards. That system became reality with the Kansas Community Junior College Act of 1965.

Dr. Barnes initiated the idea for a campus lake in 1973. He enlisted George Harshberger, an engineering instructor, and the science faculty for the project. After a dam was constructed, nature completed the job. Students initially referred to the waterway as Lake Charles for fun. The lake was renovated in 1995. After excavation work to remove years of silt deposits, the banks were stabilized, and a handicapped-accessible floating bridge was added.

Lake Charles was formally dedicated to the late Charles McDonald Barnes on May 7, 2021. Family members were on hand for the ceremony following a commencement address delivered by the 2021 Distinguished Alumnus, Dr. Roger Barnes, his son.

The lake is both a scenic area and a recreational opportunity for community fishing enthusiasts. Through an ongoing partnership, the Kansas Department of Wildlife and Parks and Tourism stocks the lake with channel catfish, crappie, largemouth bass, trout and bluegill. [56]

A Battlefield Cross, comprised of a rifle, helmet and boots, stands as a monument to three Dodge City Community College students who were killed in combat in Iraq.[57]

The bronze sculpture, located in the college quad near the Student Union, was dedicated April 23, 2008. The memorial includes a bench for each soldier bearing the following information:

Sgt. Benjamin C. Morton, US Army - Iraq, 7-10-1980 to 5-21-2005

Sgt. Christopher R. Kruse, US Army - Iraq, 4-26-1984 to 11-13-2007

L. Cpl. Brian A. Escalante, USMC - Iraq, 10-6-1981 to 2-17-2007

Sgt. Morton, from Wright, Kansas, died in Mosul when his patrol encountered enemy small arms fire. He received the Global War on Terrorism Expedition Medal; the National Defense Service Medal, The Army Good Conduct Medal; the Army Achievement Medal, and the Combat Infantryman's Badge.

Sgt. Kruse, from Dodge City, died when a makeshift bomb detonated during dismounted combat operations in Mukhisa. His awards include the National Defense Service Medal; Global War on Terrorism Service Medal; Army Service Ribbon, and Expert Infantryman Badge.

Lance Corporal Escalante, from Dodge City, was killed in Al Anbar province when a remote-controlled bomb exploded near the Humvee in which he was riding. His awards include the National Defense Service Medal, the Iraq Campaign Medal and the Global War on Terrorism Service Medal.

The Plainswoman   57

A statue commemorating the women of Dodge City was dedicated during Dodge City's centennial year on August 30, 1972. *The Plainswoman,* a steel sculpture of a frontier woman created by Earl W. (Bill) Shira III of Dodge City, was commissioned by the Womens Chamber of Commerce and the Kansas Cultural Arts Commission.

A plaque at the base of the sculpture bears the inscription:

WITH THE PERSEVERANCE OF THE
SOUTH WIND - I ESTABLISH AND
NURTURE THESE PLAINS

Sara Dyson of Dodge City penned the phrase with the subtle reference to a Native American nation. The Kansa, namesake for the State of Kansas, were known as the South Wind People.

In 1997, after weathering in the elements for twenty-five years, the steel sculpture was restored by Jim Wilson, art professor at Dodge City Community College. The restoration included hammering brass onto the exterior of the sculpture to add texture and color. The sculpture was moved from its original location in the middle of the greenway to the center of the circle drive for greater visibility.

Dodge City Women's Chamber of Commerce Memorial - Commemorative Rose Garden   58

The Memorial - Commemorative Rose Garden along 14th Avenue on the campus of Dodge City Community College was initiated by the Beautification Committee of the Women's Chamber of Commerce in 1987.

The fifty by one hundred foot garden, formally dedicated on July 16, 1987, includes raised beds with plaques identifying various species of roses. A gazebo and benches provide an opportunity for visitors to sit, relax and take time to "smell the roses."

The rose bushes are purchased by persons who want to pay tribute to a family member or friend. Names of the honorees are included on a display board at the entrance to the garden. [58]

Avenue of Flags   59
Maple Grove Cemetery

The quarter-mile Avenue of Flags is a project of the Veterans' Council. The avenue was dedicated October 16, 1977, with the placement of eight flagpoles. The project has expanded to the adjacent Greencrest Cemetery and together 475 flagpoles flank the roadways.

Patrons purchase the flags and poles in the memory of a deceased or living veteran. A plaque with the name of the honored veteran is affixed to each of the flagpoles. Government-issued casket flags are raised in this patriotic display on Memorial Day, the Fourth of July, Labor Day and Veterans Day.

Scroggins Mausoleum   60

The Arthur and Cornelia Scroggins Memorial Mausoleum was constructed in the center of the Avenue of Flags in 1981. The seventy-foot square structure, constructed by McClesky Mausoleum Company of Atlanta, Georgia, has 540 crypts and 104 niches for cremation urns. The exterior stone is Marina Pearl granite from Norway; the interior stone is Red Lavanto marble from Italy.

Arthur Scroggins was an educator. He was the principal at Coronado School in Dodge City's Mexican Village where he also taught third through sixth graders from 1929 to 1943. Over fourteen summers he traveled to fifty-seven countries. He used photographs from his world travels to enhance the education of his students in geography and history classes.

Scroggins appropriated Mark Twain's quote, "Travel is fatal to prejudice, racism, and bigotry." He was posthumously inducted into the Kansas Teachers' Hall of Fame in 2003.

A ceramic sarcophagus above the crypts of Mr. and Mrs. Scroggins depicts Arthur Scroggins in his library.

Scroggins and his wife, Cornelia, accumulated savings and invested money in real estate and the stock market. The couple structured their will to establish the Scroggins Foundation in order to provide financial support to benefit the community. The Scroggins Foundation, now part of the Community Foundation of Southwest Kansas, awards annual grants to non-profit organizations advocating for youth, education and community development. [59]

Veterans Circle   61

The Veterans Circle at Maple Grove Cemetery was dedicated on November 11, 1998. Bob Hughes, chairman of the Veterans Council, comprised of Veterans of Foreign Wars Post 1714, the American Legion, and the G.I. Forum, designed and built the memorial. The Veterans Circle stands at the site formerly occupied by the World War I stone obelisk (see page 92)

The Veterans Circle includes a sixty-foot flagpole centered in a concrete base. Positioned around the circular base are six limestone markers for the five military branches and America's Prisoners of War and Missing in Action. The Veterans Circle is the site of Dodge City's annual Veterans' Day commemoration.

Ford County Vietnam Memorial   62

The Vietnam War Memorial, inside the Veterans Circle, stands in tribute to eight Ford Countians who lost their lives in Vietnam: Seaman John R. Brock of Fort Dodge; Private First Class Richard Conrardy of Wright; Private First Class Lee Dorsey of Dodge City; Captain Charles L. Hemmingway of Dodge City; Private First Class James L. Nufer of Dodge City; Sergeant Marlen L. Phillips of Bloom; Specialist Four Frank Sanchez of Dodge City, and Sergeant Gregg Steimel of Wright.

The monument was erected on the lawn of the Ford County Courthouse in 1973. It was moved to the Veterans Circle in 1994.

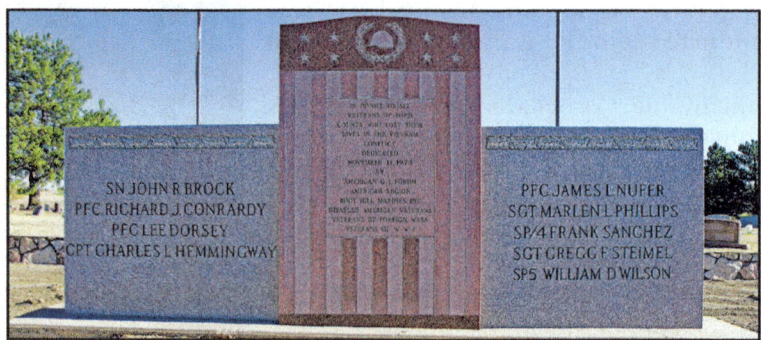

World War II Monument   63

The water fountain just outside the Veterans Circle is a World War II monument. The stone behind the fountain bears the inscription: "Dedicated in Memory of All Who served Our Country, To the Unsung Heroes Who Died of Thirst, Erected by the Mothers of World War II, Francis Black Unit 9."

The Mothers' Unit was named for the first local boy to die in World War II. Francis Black was killed in action on November 30, 1942, at Guadalcanal. The words in the dedication to "unsung heroes who died of thirst," is a reference to those United States and Filipino soldiers who died during a sixty-mile death march after their capture by the Japanese on the Bataan Peninsula.

The monument was originally erected in Wright Park and dedicated on Mother's Day, 1951. It was relocated to Maple Grove Cemetery in 2006 by Boy Scout Troop 162 to consolidate veterans memorials and provide a drinking fountain to those who visit the cemetery.

Grand Army of the Republic Monument   64

The G.A.R. section of Maple Grove Cemetery is marked by a limestone column atop a concrete and block vault. The monument, constructed in 1914 by G.A.R. Lewis Post 294, is engraved with the following epitaph:

"In Memory of Comrades That Lie In The Southland in Unmarked Graves"

Civil War relics were placed in the vault of the monument. Among them were the G.A.R. Bluebook (the roster of the 300 members of Lewis Post and the names of the twenty-four members who were living at the time of the monument's construction), a G.A.R. button, a flag and reunion programs. The limestone column is the upper portion of a damaged column originally intended for the Ford County Courthouse.

The Grand Army of the Republic was a national service organization established in 1865 by veteran Union soldiers and sailors. The group functioned to aid widows and orphans of soldiers; collect relics and erect monuments to commemorate the valor of the Union soldier. In 1911, there were 498 G.A.R. posts in Kansas. The local Post was named for Colonel William Henry Lewis, a commander at Fort Dodge, who was a casualty of the last Indian battle in Kansas near what is today Scott County Lake. [60]

Southwest Kansas Veterans Memorial   65
900 North 14th Avenue

The Southwest Kansas Veterans Memorial on the grounds of the Veterans of Foreign Wars Post 1714 includes the names of more than 650 past and present United States servicemen and women and reservists. It is the first veterans memorial in the state of Kansas that includes reserves and active military personnel.

The monument is approximately thirty-four feet long and includes four gray granite panels and three black granite panels. A Freedom Walk in front of the monument incorporates granite brick pavers with donors' names or a tribute to a veteran. Flagpoles for the American, Kansas, and POW/MIA flags surmount the monument.

The project, initiated by VFW Post 1714 and Ziegler Funeral Home, was dedicated on Memorial Day 2006. Additional names can be engraved on the monument at any time. [61]

Central School   66
1100 Central Avenue

Central School was constructed in 1927. The architect was Mann and Company of Hutchinson, Kansas; the builder was Sharp Brothers of Kansas City, Missouri. An ornate entryway and massive tower dominate the structure. Distinct design features are the decorative stonework quoining and pointed Gothic arches. Central School was designated a city landmark in 1980 as an example of collegiate Gothic architecture.

An 34,825 square foot addition, designed to complement the original architecture was completed in 2018. The addition was designed by GLMV Architecture of Wichita, Kansas; Hutton Construction of Wichita was the builder.

First Baptist Church   67
1310 Second Avenue

The First Baptist Church was constructed in 1930 under the direction of Rev. Bernard Guy. The architect was Mann and Company of Hutchinson, Kansas; the builder was Empire Construction Company of Dodge City. The brick structure is enhanced by decorative stonework.

The massive bell tower over the main entrance houses the congregation's original church bell. The bell, cast from an alloy with high silver content, is five feet high and five feet in diameter at the mouth.

The Baptist congregation was organized in 1879 and worshiped in the Union Church at First and Spruce streets. In 1884, the congregation constructed it first church at Sixth Avenue and Cedar Street under the direction of Rev. N.G. Collins. Rev. Collins was chaplain to General Ulysses S. Grant during the Civil War. He was known as the church building preacher. The Baptist Church in Dodge City was his one hundredth church.

Comanche Middle School   68
1601 First Avenue

This educational facility, constructed in 1928, exhibits modern collegiate Gothic architecture. The architect was Mann and Company of Hutchinson, Kansas; the builder was J.N. Parham of Dodge City. In 2011 a complimentary addition was constructed. The designer was GLMV Architecture of Wichita, Kansas; the builder was Hutton Construction, also of Wichita.

The main entrances include iron light fixtures suspended by chains from stone gargoyles. Supporting the gray brick walls are modern buttresses. Stone quoining accents the entire building.

The structure was originally constructed for high school classes. The city's junior college, the forerunner of Dodge City Community College held classes on the third floor from 1935 to 1957. (see page 67) Dodge City High School occupied the building until 2001 before moving to a new campus at 2201 Ross Boulevard. The structure was used as an intermediate center for fifth and sixth grades before it was opened as Comanche Middle School in 2012.

Chilton Monument   69
2000 Block of Manor Drive

The Chilton Park Monument commemorates Major Robert H. Chilton as "Guardian of the Trails." Major Chilton, a military chief, and Thomas Fitzpatrick, an Indian Agent, were instrumental in negotiating treaties with the Native Americans for the security of travelers.

On September 17, 1851, outside of Fort Laramie, now in the state of Wyoming, Chilton and Fitzpatrick met with eight tribes to secure safe passage on the Oregon Trail. On July 27, 1853, they were instrumental in negotiating a similar agreement with the Comanche, Kiowa, and Apache tribes. That treaty was signed at Fort Atkinson, two miles west of what is today Dodge City, securing safe passage for travelers on the Santa Fe Trail.

At the outset of the Civil War, Major Chilton, a native of Virginia, resigned from the United States Army. He served as chief of staff to General Robert E. Lee and as inspector general of the Army of Northern Virginia. After the war, Chilton was president of a manufacturing company in Columbus, Georgia. He died February 18, 1879, and is buried at Hollywood Cemetery in Richmond, Virginia. [62]

Chilton Park, an sixteen-acre expanse along Manor Drive between Comanche and Soule streets, was deeded to the City of Dodge City by the Continental Realty Company prior to the residential developments that now surround it. In addition to playground equipment, the park includes a walking path and an eighteen-hole disc golf course.

The original monument was unveiled at a dedication ceremony on May 28, 1931. It was restored and enhanced with storyboards by the local chapter of the Santa Fe Trail Association in 2018.

Santa Fe Trail Wagon Ruts   70
1900 Block of Burr Parkway

There are two sites in Ford County with Santa Fe Trail ruts listed on the National Register of Historical Places. [63] Some will be surprised that an example of Santa Fe Trail wagon ruts has been preserved in a residential area within Dodge City. The Green Hills O'Ford Addition was platted west of Chilton Park in 1962. The plat was designed with an island in the middle of a large turn-around in the 1900 Block of Burr Parkway. The island has several sets of distinct wagon ruts that went basically unnoticed until 1998. The wagon ruts were verified as tracks of the Santa Fe Dry Route, possibly tracks on the road from Fort Larned en route to Fort Mann or Fort Atkinson. The site was marked by the Santa Fe Trail Association in 2016.

Fire Bell Park   71
First Avenue and Soule Street

The bronze bell that tolled as the fire alarm in Dodge City between 1888 and into the 1940s is the center piece of Fire Bell Park. Before radio communications, the fire bell was the only way to summon help when a fire broke out.

Cast in a St. Louis foundry in 1887, the bell hung in the first city hall at Second Avenue and Trail Street and in the second city hall at Fifth Avenue and Spruce Street. After a new Fire Station was constructed at 201 Soule Street in 1996, the bell was largely forgotten. That changed in 2004 when Fire Chief Dan Williamson (2004-2007) had his firefighters retrieve the bell from the old firehouse. Plans soon developed for a park adjacent to the fire station.

Fire Bell Park stands as a tribute to all firefighters and the close ties between the fire department and the community. Bricks in the walkway in front of the bell are inscribed with the names of every fire chief and their years of service and the names of all the firefighters who have served the community since 1956. [64] The park was dedicated October 14, 2006, during Fire Prevention Week.

Hennessy Hall   72
200 San Jose Drive

Hennessy Hall was constructed in 1952 and served as the main building for Saint Mary of the Plains College, a four-year Catholic coeducational liberal arts college. The architect was Maguolo and Quick; the builder was McCarthy Brothers, both St. Louis companies. Hennessy Hall was listed on the National Register of Historic Places in 2004.

Hennessy Hall is named for the Most Rev. John J. Hennessy, the first bishop of the Catholic Diocese of Wichita. In 1912, Bishop Hennessy purchased the vacant Soule College at a site near what is now Melencamp Avenue and Frontview Drive. The Sisters of St. Joseph of Wichita operated Saint Mary of the Plains Academy, a boarding school for high school girls, at this site until a tornado destroyed the buildings on May 10, 1942. Although no one perished in the disaster, the Academy was forced to close.

A decade passed before a new Saint Mary of the Plains emerged. In 1952, the new campus opened as both a coeducational high school and college. The high school closed in 1969. The college continued until 1992.

The former campus is now maintained by the City of Dodge City as Saint Mary of the Plains Park. The gymnasium is operated as a YMCA. The college baseball field is utilized by the Dodge City Community College Conquistadors and the Dodge City A's. The campus has football and soccer fields as well as a walking path.

The offices and classrooms in Hennessy Hall are utilized by the Catholic Diocese of Dodge City, Newman University, Fort Hays State University, the Kansas Law Enforcement Center, Southwest Kansas Area Agency on Aging; Kansas Aging and Disability Center; Migrant State-wide Special Projects; Russell Child Development Center; Rural Education and Workforce Alliance; KansasWorks Workforce Center, MakerSpace, and the Saint Mary of the Plains Alumni Association.

Saint Mary of the Plains
Vietnam Veterans Memorial   73

A monument on the former Saint Mary of the Plains campus stands as a memorial to three St. Mary of the Plains High School alumni who died in combat during the Vietnam War.

Private First Class James Leo Nufer, Class of 1965, was an infantryman. He received the Bronze Star Medal for meritorious service in a combat zone. He died March 11, 1968, at the age of 20.

Private First Class Richard Conrardy, Class of 1969, was a medic. He received the Silver Star Medal for gallantry in combat. He died July 2, 1970, at the age of 19.

Sergeant Gregg Steimel, Class of 1968, was an infantryman. He received the Distinguished Service Cross for extraordinary heroism in combat. He died July 31, 1970, at the age of 19.

The monument, initiated by the St. Mary of the Plains Alumni Association, was dedicated June 12, 2020.

Cavalier Field Baseball Sculpture   74

It's Gone, the baseball sculpture at Dodge City's Cavalier Field, sets the viewer behind home plate. The umpire, catcher and batter are frozen in motion with heads aloft following an invisible baseball as it leaves the stadium. The stance and swing of the batter were fashioned after George Brett of the Kansas City Royals, (1973-1993). The sculpture was designed under the direction of Greg Gaskill, with the assistance of Roger Sherman, landscape architect from Fort Collins, Colorado. The iron work was fabricated by Lowell Tasset; stonework by Gary Esquibel.

17000 People witnessed Dodge City's Motor Cycle Races July 4

Dodge City 300 Race Track Site   75
One eighth of a mile east of Avenue P and Comanche

The history of the Dodge City 300 motorcycle race dates back to 1913 when the Dodge City Commercial Club hurriedly constructed a racetrack for motorcycle enthusiasts who had assembled in Hutchinson, Kansas, en route to the annual national convention of the Federation of American Motorcyclists in Denver, Colorado.

The success for this exhibition race lead to an application to host a national motorcycle race the following year. July 4, 1914, was chosen as the date for the first World Championship 300-Mile Motorcycle Race in Dodge City. The date was chosen to coincide with Independence Day and after the summer wheat harvest. [65]

A two mile oval track was graded and a grandstand was constructed to accommodate 2200 people. The event drew a crowd of over 17,000 spectators. The grandstand was filled and autos were parked three-quarters of a mile along the track. Several hundred motorcyclists were on the grounds.

The 1914 event was won by Glen Boyd of Denver. He completed the 300-mile race astride an Indian bike in four hours, twenty-four minutes and fifty-eight seconds. He averaged sixty-eight miles per hour and won a purse of $600.

The original series of sanctioned motorcycle races were held annually in Dodge City from 1914 to 1921, with the exception of the United States involvement of World War I (1917-1918). Races continued at other sites in Dodge City into the 1950s. Eventually, race fans left Dodge City for a race in the Black Hills of South Dakota at Sturgis. [66]

The racetrack site, now a wheat field in the northeast part of town, was commemorated with an historic marker on July 4, 2014, the centennial of the original race. Recognition of the anniversary included a motorcycle race at the Dodge City Roundup Arena.

Douglas A-26 Invader   76
Dodge City Airport Entrance

A Douglas A-26 Invader aircraft stands as a monument to the military personnel who were trained at the Dodge City Army Air Field from 1942 to 1945. The airbase, as it was called, was located six miles northwest of Dodge City on 2,520 acres. It was used exclusively as an Army Air Forces pilot school. An estimated 2,215 student officers, French nationals and Women's Air Force Service Pilots (WASPS) completed the nine-week flight training program at the base.

During Dodge City's Centennial Year, 1972, Joe Berkely, then the publisher of the *High Plains Journal,* worked to locate a suitable aircraft to stand as a reminder of the World War II pilots who were trained here. Originally, the Martin B-26 Marauder was the model flown at the airbase; later the pilots flew the Douglas A-26 Invader. The aircraft displayed at Dodge City's Airport was located in a government graveyard in Tucson, Arizona. After a few repairs and a little maintenance, Berkely, who was a flight instructor at the airbase, flew the bomber to Dodge City.

The student pilots trained in aircraft that were given historical Dodge City names that included: Wyatt Earp, Bat Masterson, Chalk Beeson, Bob Wright, Bill Tilghman, and Ham Bell. Other planes were named Boot Hill Outlaw, Boot Hill Buckaroo, Boot Hill Dust Storm, and Boot Hill Sod Buster. [67]

Dodge City Airfield 1943

Nevins Airport Terminal   77
Dodge City Regional Airport

The terminal building at Dodge City Regional Airport was constructed in 1942 as a Works Progress Administration (WPA) project. A planned dedication was postponed during World War II and largely forgotten until July 28, 1991, when the building was named the Nevins Airport Terminal. The designation honors the six children of Ozro Newton Nevins and Martha Griffith Nevins for their "life-times of achievement." [68]

Eulalia Nevins (July 3, 1882 - March 23, 1961) served as Ford County Superintendent of Public Instruction, an elected position, from 1910 to 1917. She visited each school in the county twice a year traveling by horse and buggy. From 1918 to 1947, she taught at Dodge City High School. She was instrumental in establishing Dodge City Junior College in 1935. She was posthumously inducted into the Kansas Teachers Hall of Fame in 1983.

Clarence Nevins (December 9, 1886 - May 25, 1961) served as state director of the Works Progress Administration from 1937 to 1943. He was responsible for overseeing projects throughout the state that provided employment to needy Kansans during the Depression. Among the projects in Dodge City were the Bandshell, McCarthy Stadium and additions to the Hoover Pavilion in Wright Park, the Carnegie Library, and the terminal at the airport.

Arthur Nevins (March 29, 1895 - September 24, 1978) served as mayor of Dodge City from 1936 to 1942. During his tenure, the municipal airport was constructed. He was instrumental in acquiring land, the construction of runways, quarrying stone for the terminal, building hangers and working with the federal government and airlines to bring commercial aviation to Dodge City. He served two terms as State Representative from Ford County (1953-1956).

Ralph Nevins (April 24, 1896 - November 25, 1950) was heavily involved in the family hardware business. Nevins Hardware had stores in Dodge City, Kinsley, Ford and Ensign. When the United States entered World War I, he enlisted and was sent overseas. He suffered respiratory complications due to mustard gassing. He was a member of the American Legion, the Veterans of Foreign Wars and had an intense interest in Boy Scout work.

Dr. Irmagene Nevins Holloway (August 7, 1899 - September 12, 2000) served as head of the Department of Health/Physical Education for Women; and Safety Education for Women at Pittsburg State University. She served as National Director of Accident Prevention for the American Red Cross in Washington, D.C. She also established driver education training as a course in Kansas high schools.

Elizabeth Nevins Soulen (July 19, 1904 - November 23, 1986) was a teacher, church and community leader. She married Dr. Harold Soulen, a Methodist minister, and served as district president of the Women's Society of Christian Service and was on the executive committee of the Board of Missions for the Methodist Church. She was also director of public relations at St. Paul's Theological Seminary in Kansas City, Missouri. [69]

Landmarks in Ford County Outside of Dodge City

Point of Rocks
Three miles west of Dodge City on U.S. 50

Point of Rocks was a major landmark on the Santa Fe Trail. It served as a campsite and an elevated spot to view the vast prairie. Until 1848, travelers facing south were looking across the Arkansas River into Mexico. The bluff extended further south but its prominence was altered by road construction projects in 1981 and 2023. The Santa Fe Trail Association advocated that this historic site not be destroyed due to its historic value. The remaining segment of Point of Rocks was secured and stabilized for its historic significance.

Circa 1906

Caches, Fort Mann, Camp Mackey,
Fort Atkinson, Post Office sites
U.S. 50 and 107 Road

In 1926, a marker was erected in two miles west of Dodge City on U.S. 50 commemorating a number of sites along the Santa Fe Trail. Highway construction forced the marker's relocation and reconstruction in 1936 and 2023.

The Caches originated when the James Baird and Samuel Chambers' pack train was overcome by a blizzard in 1823. [70] The Santa Fe traders were stranded for three months and most of their animals perished during the severe winter. In the spring, before leaving for New Mexico to purchase other pack animals, the party dug chambers in the ground to hide their trade goods. After they returned to retrieve the goods, the caches become noticeable and the site became a popular campsite for travelers on the Santa Fe Trail.

Fort Mann was constructed in 1847, not far from Caches. The fort was used as a rest and repair depot for government wagon trains. It was named for Captain Daniel Mann, a master teamster. The fort, consisting of four log houses and a stockade, was abandoned in 1850.

That same year, Camp Mackey was established further west of the Fort Mann site. Government troops were stationed here to protect travelers from Indian raids. The structures at this post were constructed of stacked sod and tent canvases. The camp was named for Colonel Aeneas Mackey, but later renamed Fort Atkinson in honor of Colonel Henry Atkinson.

Fort Atkinson was the site of the signing of an 1853 Indian treaty. Major Robert H. Chilton, commanding officer, and Thomas "Broken-Hand" Fitzpatrick, a federal Indian agent, drafted the treaty for the security of those on the Santa Fe Trail. (see page 77) Fort Atkinson was abandoned as a military post that same year, but it functioned as a post office from 1854 to 1857. [71]

The Wet-Dry Chapter of the Santa Fe Trail Association marked the individual locations with limestone posts, bronze plaques and storyboards: Caches – 10692 107 Road; Fort Mann – 10761 Kettle Way and Fort Atkinson – west of 10730 Kettle Way.

Circa 1925

Santa Fe Trail Remains
Nine miles west of Dodge City on U.S. 50/U.S. 400

The Santa Fe Trail was utilized predominately between 1822 and 1872 as a freight road. Use of the trail reached its peak in 1847, when 9,884 wagons pulled by 98,840 mules, horses and oxen carried 59,304,000 pounds of merchandise the distance between Independence, Missouri, and Santa Fe. The use of the trail dwindled in 1872 when the westward expansion of the railroad reached Colorado.

The width of the trail varied from a few feet to a quarter of a mile in places. Heavy freight wagons dug their wheels deep into the earth, hindering travel for smaller wagons built lower to the ground. When the roadway became too muddy and the ruts too deep, the wagoneers moved their teams to the side and followed the trail on dryer ground.

The Santa Fe Trail Remains site was designated a National Historic Landmark in 1966. A highway turn off enables travelers to view a visible stretch of the Santa Fe Trail. A kiosk and storyboards along a boardwalk provide a look into the nineteenth century when travel wasn't measured in hours but days.

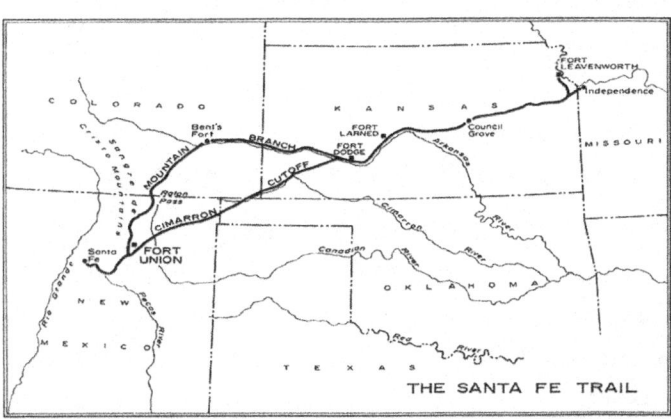

THE SANTA FE TRAIL

Fort Dodge
Five miles east of Dodge City on U.S. 400

Fort Dodge was established in 1865 as an important military post on the Santa Fe Trail. It was abandoned by the military in 1882. The facility has served as the Kansas Soldiers' Home since 1890. Many of the buildings constructed for the military post in 1867 are still used today.

Fort Dodge is a community of veterans and veterans' dependents spread out over seventy acres. Housing includes sixty cottages, three dormitories and an eighty-six-bed nursing care facility.

Looking much like a small town, Fort Dodge includes a sutler's store and cafe, a U.S. Post Office, a chapel, a library-museum, and an administration building with an auditorium and recreation center. The unincorporated town also has a park and picnic area with a display of war memorials and a fishing pond for residents.

Custer House

Halsey Hall

Nimitz Hall

Post Office

87

Kansas Soldiers' Home Cemetery
Five miles east of Dodge City on U.S. 400

The Kansas Soldiers' Home Cemetery dates back to 1890 when Fort Dodge was deeded to the State of Kansas for use as a veterans' home. The cemetery is the final resting place of veterans, spouses and civilians who resided at the Kansas Soldiers' Home. When the cemetery was entered in the Register of Historic Kansas Places in 2007, the veterans' interments were listed by era: Civil War, 655; Indian Wars, four; Mexican War, three; Spanish-American War, 104; World War I, 141; World War II, 143; Korean War, thirteen; and Vietnam War, five. [72]

The Kansas Veterans' Cemetery at Fort Dodge, adjacent to the Kansas Soldiers' Home Cemetery, was established in 2002. The cemetery has burial spaces for more than 600 veterans and eligible dependents. There are two columbarium walls with 320 niches for cremation urns and another 1,263 sites for in-ground cremation interments. There is also a garden for scattering ashes. The cemetery includes a covered shelter for burial services. Three other Kansas Veterans' cemeteries are located in WaKeeney, Winfield and Fort Riley.

Coronado Cross and Historical Park
Six miles east of Dodge City on U.S. 400

Francisco Vasquez de Coronado; Father Juan de Padilla, a Franciscan friar; and thirty conquistadores set out from Mexico in 1540 to search for the gold of the Seven Cities of Cibola.

On June 29, 1541, the entourage crossed what is now known as the Arkansas river east of present-day Dodge City. They named the waterway *El Rio de San Pedro y San Pablo*, having crossed it on the feast of Saints Peter and Paul. On a hill above the turbulent river, Father Padilla offered a Mass of thanksgiving.

A thirty-eight-foot cross constructed by Pre-Stressed Concrete Company of Newton, Kansas, was erected by the Ford County Historical Society to memorialize the first Christian service in the area. The State of Kansas and the National Bicentennial Committee named the Coronado Historical Park an official bicentennial project. The park was officially dedicated on July 4, 1976, honoring those of American Indian, Mexican and Spanish heritages.

The land for the ten-acre park was donated by the Karl Miller family. Miller served the community as district judge from 1922 to 1955. He studied the history of Coronado's expeditions and determined that his ranch had been crossed by the ancient travelers.

Battle of Coon Creek Site
Leander Herron's Medal of Honor
Jewell Road and 125 Road, 1/2 mile south

Corporal Leander Herron, a soldier at Fort Dodge and Fort Larned, was awarded the Congressional Medal of Honor for his actions during a September 2, 1868, Indian battle in Ford County.

Corporal Herron and Corporal Patrick Boyle were headed to Fort Larned with a mail dispatch when they came upon four soldiers under attack by nearly fifty Kiowa Indians. The detail was gathering wood along the meandering Coon Creek eleven miles northeast of Fort Dodge.

Boyle, having the faster horse, headed back to Fort Dodge for reinforcements; Herron stayed with the detail. The soldiers pushed their wagon into a deep buffalo wallow and took cover beneath it. They were able to hold off every charge made by the Kiowas until a company from the fort forced their retreat.

Herron wrote an account about the Battle of Coon Creek that was reprinted in newspapers across the nation. His story caught the attention of someone who convinced Congress to award Herron the Congressional Medal of Honor in 1917. Patrick Boyle, just as deserving, died in 1913.

The site of the Battle of Coon Creek is on private property and is posted. A storyboard, erected by the local chapter of the Santa Fe Trail Association can be viewed from the road. [73]

Fort Hays - Fort Dodge Military Road Marker
Southeast Corner of Ford County/Hodgeman County Line and U.S. 283

The Sawlog Creek Crossing on the Fort Hays - Fort Dodge Road is located at the northern edge of Ford County. A nearly three-mile unbroken stretch of intact swales along with the crossing of Sawlog Creek is listed on the National Register of Historic Places. The site is on private property and not accessible. The seventy-five mile Fort Hays - Fort Dodge Road was an important secondary route of the Santa Fe Trail. The road was established in 1867 when the Union Pacific Railroad reached Hays. Military freight, commercial freight, along with mail and passengers, traveled by rail to Hays and then by wagon or stage to the main branch of the Santa Fe Trail near Fort Dodge. Travel on the Fort Hays - Fort Dodge Road ended in 1872 when the Atchison, Topeka and Santa Fe Railroad reached Dodge City. [74] The monument at right, located one half mile east of the aforementioned corner on Antelope Road, marks the beginning of the swales. Designed as a flagpole, the monument was constructed by the landowner of concrete from an old silo and a tightly wound ball of barbed wire. The corner marker at the highway is a storyboard.

Fort Dodge - Camp Supply Military Road Marker
nine miles south of Dodge City on US 283

The southeast corner of U.S. 283 and Upland Road includes several markers recognizing the importance of the area. The ninety-mile military road between Fort Dodge and Camp Supply, the Great Western Cattle Trail, and the Mulberry Creek Crossing of the Santa Fe Trail all converged at this site. The Jones and Plummer Trail, a route to Fort Elliot, Texas, and the road to Tascosa, Texas, also crossed the Mulberry Creek at this site. Dugan's Road House, a store and way station, was located in the vicinity on the north bank of Mulberry Creek. [75]

Fowler's Ruts and Black Pool
Southwest Corner of Ridge Road and 129th Road

Officially known as Santa Fe Trail - Ford County Segment 2, Fowler's Ruts and Black Pool, are located approximately four miles northeast of the town of Ford. The trail segment, listed on the National Register of Historic Places and named for the landowner, includes four swales and a spring mentioned in historic-period diaries. Black Pool is deep and has a dark coloration due to the underlying strata of black shale. Carved names and initials in the rock surrounding the pool provide evidence that the area was used as a Santa Fe Trail campsite. A Santa Fe Trail Association marker a quarter mile to the east of the intersection on Jewell Road recognizes the September 5, 1825, campsite of the George Champlin Sibley survey team that mapped the trail from Fort Osage, Missouri to Santa Fe. The site is on private property and not accessible to the public. [76]

Immaculate Heart of Mary Church, Windthorst
Jewell Road and 131 Spur Road

Immaculate Heart of Mary Church, a Gothic Romanesque Revival edifice, was designed by Preuss and Aimes of St. Louis, Missouri. The builder, William Foley of Dodge City, constructed the church between 1912 and 1913. The stained glass windows depicting scenes from the New Testament were designed by Emil Frei Studios of St. Louis and installed in 1916.

The red brick structure includes yellow brick crosses in the center of the bell tower and at the corners of the gabled walls. A statue of the Blessed Virgin Mary stands in the niche above the main entrance. The eight-sided steeple, topped with a golden cross, stands approximately 125 feet in height and can be seen at a distance of seven miles. The interior of the church is ornate with statuary and a canopy baldachin over the main altar.

The community was founded in 1878 when a group of German families immigrated from Cincinnati, Ohio. The unincorporated farming community was named for Ludwig von Windthorst, the leader of a Catholic Centre Political Party, who at the time was fighting in the German homeland, against the policies of Otto von Bismarck, to protect the Church from state domination.

Immaculate Heart of Mary Parish was closed in 1997. The church is listed on the National Register of Historic Places and is maintained by the Windthorst Heritage Association.

Former Landmarks

Immaculate Heart of Mary Chapel - When St. Mary of the Plains College closed in 1992, the chapel became a secular space and the religious art was removed. The statue of the Blessed Virgin Mary outside the chapel was sent to Wichita where it was placed in a courtyard at the Sisters of St. Joseph motherhouse. The Emil Frei stained glass windows were incorporated in the design of the motherhouse chapel constructed in 1995. The Our Lady of the Plains altar mural and limestone statues of Mary and Joseph were transferred to Sacred Heart Cathedral in Dodge City. The marble altar was disassembled and reconstructed at St. Andrew's Church in Wright, Kansas. The pipe organ was purchased by Trinity Lutheran Church in Garden City, Kansas.

Great War Monument - An eight-sided stone pinnacle, constructed in 1938 as a work project of the National Youth Administration, stood thirty-two feet high in Maple Grove Cemetery. An attached plaque read: In Honor of Those Who Answered Their Country's Call in the Great War, 1917-1918. World War I was called the Great War until there was a World War II. The stone pinnacle was damaged beyond repair after a lightning strike on April 19, 1997. The monument was replaced by a sixty-foot flagpole surrounded with commemorative markers. (see Veterans' Circle page 72)

Milburn Stone Theatre - The theatre at Saint Mary of the Plains College (SMPC) was named for Kansas-native Milburn Stone, the actor who portrayed Doc Adams in the television series *Gunsmoke*. Stone received a honorary Doctorate of Philosophy in Humane Letters from the institution in 1976. After Stone's death on June 12, 1980, the Plains Playhouse was renamed and an exhibit was constructed with his personal memorabilia. When SMPC closed in 1992, Mrs. Jane Stone donated the collection to the National Cowboy and Western Heritage Museum in Oklahoma City.

McCarty Stadium - As early as 1905, plat maps showed a racetrack in Wright Park. The course was utilized for horse, motorcycle and stock car races. In 1939, WPA workers replaced the wooden grandstands with a concrete stadium. The stadium was named for Thomas L. McCarty, the first doctor to practice in Dodge City. McCarthy practiced medicine for fifty-eight years before his death on April 2, 1930. McCarthy Stadium was a popular dirt track that drew racers and fans to Dodge City from Colorado, Oklahoma and throughout Kansas on Saturday nights during the summer months. The aging facility was demolished in 2006, six years after the opening of Dodge City Raceway Park at 11322 110 Road.

Sitler-Bell Building - Once a designated landmark, the vacant Sitler-Bell Building deteriorated and eventually collapsed in 1989. The building, formerly located at 309 West Trail Street, was noted for its architectural style that was typical of brick structures erected on the north side of Front Street in 1886. The metal cornice and cast-iron porch were common features of that era. Originally, Ham Bell operated a furniture store and undertaker's supply house on the first floor, using the second floor as his residence. After Bell sold the building, it was a hotel and house of ill repute, a grocery, printing and office supply business and an antique store.

Water Plant - The history of the city's water system dates back to 1886 when the Wichita firm of J.A. Jones pumped water from the Arkansas River and filtered it through a half mile of sand and gravel. When water became a city utility in 1910, the water plant was constructed at 703 West Trail. The building with its flattened roof and extended eaves had design features similar to Prairie Style architecture. The structure was destroyed by fire on April 15, 2021. The city obtains its water from twenty-five wells in the Ogallala Aquifer.

Photo/Graphic Credits

In addition to the photographs taken by Gentry Heimerman, photographs and graphics are attributed by page.

p. 7 – West cowboy silhouettes, *Dodge City Daily Globe*

p. 9 – Boot Hill logo, Boot Hill Museum

p. 10 – Boot Hill 1937; Boot Hill Circa 1953, Kansas Heritage Center

p. 11 – Future site of Front Street Replica. Circa 1954, courtesy Kirk Hendricks

p. 11 – Front Street Replica, Circa 1963, Boot Hill Museum

p. 12 – Boot Hill Cemetery, undated, Boot Hill Museum

p. 12 – Boot Hill – Front Street Replica, 1977, Troy Robinson

p. 14 – Colonel R.J. Hardesty, Kansas Heritage Center

p. 19 – Hiram T. Burr, *Dodge City Daily Globe*

p. 20 – Buffalo head sculpture, Noel Ary

p. 21 – Dr. O.H. Simpson, Kansas State Historical Society

p. 22 – Hamilton B. Bell, Kansas Heritage Center

p. 23 – Dennis Hopper astride motorcycle, artist conception, Janet Zoble

p. 28 – Variety Store, Kansas Heritage Center

p. 29 – *El Capitán,* author

p. 32 – Dennis Weaver star, author

p. 33 – Land Acquisition map, Michael Snapp

p. 35 – Historic view of sundials, Kansas State Historical Society

p. 36 – Santa Fe Reading Room, Kansas Heritage Center

p. 38 – Fort Dodge cornerstone, Noel Ary

p. 39 – *Dodge City* World Premiere, Kansas Heritage Center

p. 40 – Beeson Theatre 1930, Kansas Heritage Center; 1986, author

p. 41 – Dodge City Cowboy Band, Chalk Beeson, Kansas Heritage Center

p. 44 – First School Site plaque, Noel Ary

p. 45 – Union Church on Gospel Hill, Kansas Heritage Center

p. 52 – *Crucifixion on Calvary,* Mark Dunkle

p. 54 – Robert Wright, Kansas State Historical Society

p. 55 – Wright-Mootz Memorial, author

p. 56 – Dodge City Flour Mill, Flour Sack, Kansas Heritage Center

p. 57 – Lone Sentinel, Farrow Ford; plaque, Noel Ary

p. 58 – Bridge photos, Kansas Heritage Center; plaque, Noel Ary

p. 59 – Municipal Bandshell, author

p. 60 – George M. Hoover, Kansas State Historical Society

p. 64 – Sod House and H.L. Sitler, Kansas State Historical Society; plaque, Noel Ary

p. 68 – Dr. Charles Barnes, Dodge City Community College

p. 71 – Avenue of Flags; Ceramic Sarcophagus, author

p. 73 – World War II Monument; Grand Army of the Republic Monument, author

p. 77 – Santa Fe Trail Wagon Ruts, author

p. 80 – Dodge City 300 Motorcycle Race, Kansas Heritage Center

p. 83 – Point of Rocks: *Dodge City Daily Globe,* courtesy Stan Trekell, Great Western Trail Association

p. 85 – Santa Fe Trail Remains, Kansas State Historical Society; map Kansas Heritage Center; plaque, Noel Ary

p. 89 – Leander Herron, National Park Service

p. 90 – Road Markers, author

p. 91 – Black Pool and Windthorst Church, author

p. 92, 93 – All photos, author

Endnotes

1. Leo Olivia, *Fort Dodge: Sentry of the Western Plains*, p. 17.

2. There were tents and a few wooden structures already constructed in June of 1872 before the Dodge City Town Company was formally organized on August 15, 1872.

3. Colonel Dodge's wartime rank was Lieutenant Colonel but generally known as Colonel Dodge as a courtesy title though while at Fort Dodge, his rank was Major. On his official correspondence, he continued to refer to himself as Major Dodge.

4. Fredric Young, *The Delectable Burg*, p . 13: "Before Robert M. Wright died he told Heinie Schmidt, amateur historian and son of an early Dodge City blacksmith, that the founding group met in Wright's sutler's store at Fort Dodge. A name to replace 'Buffalo City' was discussed, and all agreed that it should be 'Dodge City' in honor of Major Richard I. Dodge. 'After all,' Wright said, 'the Colonel is the fort's commandant, we have just named him as president of our town company, and because of his help, he has encouraged some of his officers to put up some cash and join us founders and stockholders. We will call this company 'The Dodge City Town Company' in his honor.' Commander Dodge agreed to the name 'Dodge City' but insisted that if anyone ever asked, to tell them it was named after the fort. So let it stand—-Dodge City was named for a fort, not a person."

5. Robert Dykstra and Jo Ann Manfra's *Dodge City and the Birth of the West*, p. 183 lists twenty-four homicides in Dodge City from 1872-1878.

6. The structure was constructed and is identified as the Municipal Building on the National Register of Historic Places.

7. Odie Faulk, *Dodge City, The Most Western Town of All*, p. 151 notes there were approximately thirty mounds of earth on Boot Hill, p. 151.

8. *Dodge City Daily Globe*, February 21, 1947.

9. *Dodge City Daily Globe*, September 10, 1947.

10. Troy Robinson, *People and Places of Dodge City, Volume II*, p. 116.

11. Nomination forms for the Kansas Cowboy Hall of Fame are available at Boothill.org

12. Robert Haywood, *Trails South*, pgs. 102-103.

13. www.stephenfried.com/blog/?=p1733, accessed December 20, 2022.

14. *Dodge City Daily Globe*, August 16, 2021.

15. Burr House, National Register registration form Section 8, pages 5 and 6, December 4, 2007

16. Troy Robinson, *People and Places of Dodge City, Volume II*, p. 96. Bill's Tavern, a bar located on Chestnut Street, was especially popular during World War II when the Dodge City Airbase was open west of town.

17. Oxen were steers of various breeds that were trained as draft animals to pull wagons.

18. *Dodge City Journal*, April 4, 1935.

19. *Dodge City Daily Globe*, December 23, 2019.

20. *Dodge City Journal*, May 29, 1930.

21. National Register registration form for Dodge City's Historic District pages 63 and 64, November 4, 2009.

22. Gary and Margaret Kraisinger, *The Western, The Greatest Texas Cattle Trail*, 1874 - 1886, p. 297.

23. Acreage figured from article in the *Dodge City Daily Globe*, November 9, 1935.

24. www.acatholicmission.org/9-the-osage-leave-kansas, accessed January 13, 2023

25. The Trail of Fame Inductees as of 2022.

26. Santa Fe Depot, National Register application, June 2, 2000.

27. *Dodge City Globe*, January 5, 1917.

28. *Dodge City Daily Globe*, March 17, 1947. Henry Ikeda worked for ATSF from 1912 until his death on March 17, 1947.

29. *Dodge City's Mexican Village, A Place in Time*, by Tim Wenzl.

30. *Dodge City Daily Globe*, December 31, 1929, and *Dodge City Journal*, January 9, 1930.

31. Newsreel coverage of the premiere of "Dodge City" can be viewed at www.youtube.com/watch?v=zuP-vur09ro

32. *Dodge City Daily Globe*, January 28, 2017, Martha Muncy obituary.

33. Names of actors recorded in the April 2, 1939 editions of the *Kansas City Star*, *Wichita Beacon*, and the *Hutchinson Herald*.

34. http://www.kansashistory.us/fordco/churches, accessed March 27, 2023.

35. *Dodge City Times*, April 13, 1878.

36. Odie Faulk, *Dodge City, The Most Western Town of All*, p. 174. Tom Nixon had recently replaced Dave Mather in the position of assistant marshal. The two became bitter enemies. On July 18, 1884, Nixon shot at Mather claiming he had drawn first. Three days later Mather shot and killed Nixon. "The weight of the testimony showed that Nixon was the aggressor in the affray and that Mather was justified in shooting." Nixon was acquitted by the jury. *Dodge City Times*, January 8, 1885, quoting the *Kinsley Graphic*. The trial took place in the District Court at Kinsley, Kansas.

37. *Dodge City Daily Globe*, November 10, 1927.

38. *Dodge City Journal*, May 23, 1929.

39. Ida Ellen Rath, *Early Ford County*, p. 17.

40. Robert Baughman, Kansas Post Offices, p. 45. The dates of the post office at Fort Atkinson are recorded as November 11, 1851 to August 22, 1853.

41. ibid, p. 46. After the post office was transferred to Dodge City in 1872, a post office was reestablished at Fort Dodge from 1876 to 1882 and has operated there since 1893.

42. *Dodge City Globe*, June 14, 2022.

43. National Register registration form for Dodge City's Historic District #19, November 4, 2009.

44. *Dodge City Daily Globe*, September 29, 2012 and December 17, 2013.

45. The Daughters of the American Revolution placed six Santa Fe Trail markers in Ford County. The locations for all of the markers throughout the state of Kansas can be found at www.santafetrailresearch.com/research/dar-marker-location-ks.html

46. *Dodge City Journal*, July 25, 1929.

47. www.kansashistory.us/fordco/hoover.html, accessed February 26, 2023.

48. www.nps.gov/flni/learn/historyculture/flight93story.htm, accessed March 11, 2023.

49. www.britannica.com, September 11, 2001 Terrorist Attack, accessed March 11, 2023

50. Additions were constructed from 1911 to 1932 when the building gained its current form.

51. Kansas Power Company Plant, Register of Historic Kansas Places application, pg. 16, August 13, 2016.

52. *Ford County Directory for 1942* published by the Southwest Kansas Credit Association, Dodge City.

53. *Dodge City Daily Globe,* December 9, 2016.

54. *Los Angeles Times,* July 22, 2016.

55. *The Conquistador,* Fall 2020 issue, pgs. 4-9.

56. *The Conquistador,* Summer 2021 issue, pgs. 14-15.

57. *The Conquistador,* April 30, 2008 issue, pgs. 1, 5.

58. For information about how to purchase a rose bush, contact the Women's Chamber of Commerce at P.O. Box 351, Dodge City, KS 67801.

59. Grant and scholarship applications can be found at www.communityfoundationswks.com

60. Officially known as The Battle of Punished Woman's Fork at Battle Canyon. For more information see www.legendsofamerica.com/battle-punished-woman-fork-kansas/

61. For information about adding veterans' names to the memorial, contact the Dodge City VFW post, 909 N 13th Avenue, Dodge City KS, 67801. (620) 225-7081.

62. www.santafetrail.org/pdf/Robert-Hall-Chilton, accessed February, 20, 2023

63. The National Register of Historic Places lists two Santa Fe wagon ruts sites in Ford County: Santa Fe Trail Remains on page 85 and Fowler's Ruts and Black Pool on page 91.

64. Records of fire department personnel were only available starting in 1956.

65. Troy Robinson, *People and Places of Dodge City, Volume II,* pgs. 117-120.

66. Text from Dodge City 300 storyboard on site.

67. *Dodge City Daily Globe,* July 3, 1943 and September 2, 1943.

68. *Dodge City Daily Globe,* July 26, 1991.

69. Tim Wenzl, unpublished manuscript entitled "A Family of Service, The Nevins Family of Dodge City," 1991.

70. In a book of collected articles entitled *Matt Field on the Santa Fe Trail,* the year the Caches were dug is cited on page 129 as 1822.

71. Robert Baughman, *Kansas Post Offices* records the years for the post office at Fort Atkinson as 1851 to 1853, p.45

72. Kansas Soldiers Home Cemetery, Register of Historic Kansas Places application dated December 4, 2007.

73. Storyboard text by Leo Olivia, former professor of history at Fort Hays State University.

74. Fort Hays – Fort Dodge Military Road, National Register of Historic Places Registration Form dated July 17, 2013.

75. A storyboard and two concrete posts are on site.

76. National Register of Historic Places Registration Form dated July 17, 2013.

Bibliography

BOOKS

Blackmar, Frank W. *Kansas*. Chicago: Standard Publishing Company, 1912

Connelley, William E. *Kansas and Kansans*. Chicago: Lewis Publishing Co., 1919

Davis, Kenneth Sydney. *Kansas: A Bicentennial History*. New York: Norton, 1976

Dodge City, Ford County, Kansas. Dodge City: Fred A. Etrick Printery Museum, 1887.

Diamond Jubilee, 1885-1960. Dodge City: Sacred Heart Cathedral Parish, 1960.

Dykstra, Robert and Jo Ann Manfra. *Dodge City and the Birth of the West*. Lawrence, Kansas: University of Kansas Press, 2017.

Faulk, Odie B. *Dodge City: The Most Western Town of All*. New York: Oxford University Press, 1977.

Fletcher, Sir Banister. *A History of Architecture*. New York: Charles Scribner's Sons, 1961.

Hamlin Talbot Faulkner. *The American Spirit in Architecture*. New Haven: Yale University Press, 1926.

Haywood, C. Robert. *Trails South*. Norman, Oklahoma: University of Oklahoma Press, 1986.

Kraisinger, Gary and Margaret. *The Western, The Greatest Texas Cattle Trail, 1874 – 1886*. Newton, Kansas: Mennonite Press, 2004

Porter, Clyde and Mae Reed. *Matt Field on the Santa Fe Trail*. Norman, Oklahoma: University of Oklahoma Press, 1960

Rath, Ida Ellen. *Early Ford County*. Newton, Kansas: Mennonite Press, 1964.

_____. *The Rath Trail*. Wichita, Kansas: McCormick-Armstrong Co., 1961.

Richmond, Robert N. *Kansas: A Land of Contrasts*. St. Charles, Mo.: Forum Press, 1974.

Robinson, Troy. *People and Places of Dodge City*. Spearville, Kansas: Spearville News, 2011.

_____. *People and Places of Dodge City, Volume II*. Spearville, Kansas: Spearville News, 2017.

Rydjord, John. *Kansas Place-Names*. Norman: University of Oklahoma Press, 1972.

Schmidt, Heinie. *Ashes of My Campfire*. Dodge City: Journal, Inc., 1952.

Socolofsky, Homer E., and Huber Self. *Historical Atlas of Kansas*. Norman: University of Oklahoma Press, 1972.

Strate, David K. *Sentinel to the Cimarron: The Frontier Experience of Fort Dodge, Kansas*. Dodge City: Cultural Heritage and Arts Center, 1970.

Watkins, Ethel and Jennie Burrichter. *Our First Century (1878-1978), An Historical Sketch*. Dodge City: First Presbyterian Church, 1978.

Wenzl, Tim. *Dodge City's Mexican Village, A Place in Time, 1906-1956*. Amazon: CreateSpace, 2022.

Wheeler, Keith. *The Townsmen*. Alexandra, Va.: Time-Life, Inc, 1975.

Young, Fredric R. *Dodge City: Up Through a Century in Story and Pictures*. Dodge City: Boot Hill Museum, Inc., 1972.

_____. *The Delectable Burg, An Irreverent History of Dodge City, 1872 to 1886*. Dodge City: Kansas Heritage Center, 2009.

Zornow, William Frank, *Kansas: A History of the Jayhawk State*. Norman: University of Oklahoma Press, 1957.

NEWSPAPERS/MAGAZINES

Dodge City Community College Conquistador
Dodge City Daily Globe
Dodge City Democrat
Dodge City Journal
Dodge City Times

Ford County Globe
Ford County Globe Republican
High Plains Journal
Hutchinson News
Legend Magazine

ARTICLES

Howes, Cecil. "Opening of the Santa Fe Trail," Kansas Teacher, (March 1948), 46-48

Lyons, Sam B. "Belt Buckle Banking of Kansas: Dodge City's Fidelity State Bank Combines Old-Fashioned Hospitality with Modern Banking Procedures," Finance, March 15, 1948, 27-29, 48.

"Santa Fe Trail: Brief Summary of the Santa Fe Trail through Kansas," Eighteenth Biennial Report of the Kansas State Historical Society, 1911-1912, (1913), 1-21.

"Wings Over Kansas: Dodge City Army Air Field," Kansas Historical Quarterly, XXV (Summer 1959), 135-38.

Westermeier, Clifford P. "The Dodge City Cowboy Band," Kansas Historical Quarterly, XIX (February 1951), 1-11.

OTHER SOURCES

Covalt, Jeanie. "Peace Officers of Dodge City, 1873 to 1979." Kansas Heritage Center, 1979.

Dodge City Commission Minutes.

Ford County Register of Deeds Records.

Lane, Larry N. "J.C. Denious: Public Servant and State Promoter of Southwestern Kansas." History Series No. 5 (October 1968), Fort Hays State.

Trauer, Nancy Jo. "Dodge City History." Dodge City Public Library, 1978.

Wiggans, Owens D. "A History of Dodge City," M.A. Thesis, Colorado State College of Education. Greeley, Colorado, 1938.

"Will of Robert M. Wright," Ford County District Court Files, 1915.

Vertical Files, Kansas Heritage Center, Dodge City.

Subject Index

About the Author – Tim Wenzl

A Kansas City, Missouri native, Tim moved to Dodge City in 1977 after landing his first "real" job upon graduating from University of Missouri – Columbia. As a reporter for the *Dodge City Daily Globe*, he became fascinated with the history that surrounded him. He published his first book "Discovering Dodge City's Landmarks" in 1980. He worked for St. Mary of the Plains College as director of public relations, and for the Catholic Diocese of Dodge City as the editor of the *Southwest Kansas Register* and then diocesan archivist. He was named archivist emeritus upon his retirement in 2017. He enjoys the discovery of research and preserving history before it is lost to time. This is his twenty-third book.

Contact the author at twenzl@dcdiocese.org

About the Photographer – Gentry Heimerman

In 2015, Gentry and his beloved wife Sydney were married in Hays, Kansas. Within a few short months they began working in Dodge City, bought a home, and discovered that "Baby Theo" was on his way. Seemingly in the blink of an eye, three more children (Hattie, Aidan, and Ezra) have come along. His contributions in this book are dedicated to them, and to his mother, Kari Heimerman, a talented photographer who has passed down a love for capturing the beautiful. Gentry currently serves as the Director of Young Adult Ministry for the Catholic Diocese of Dodge City, and is a proud alumnus of Fort Hays State University and the University of Notre Dame. *Ad Majorem Dei Gloriam*

Categorized Historic Buildings, Sites

Dodge City Designated Landmarks

Brick Streets - 17
Burr House - 19
Carnegie Arts Center - 25
Central School - 74
Dodge Theatre Building - 39
Fidelity State Bank - 28
Ford County Courthouse - 46
Hardesty House - 14
Hennessy Hall - 78
Hinkle-Heinz House - 50

Home of Stone - 48
Hoover Pavilion - 60
Lora-Locke Hotel - 38
Municipal Building – 20
Post Office – 47
Presbyterian Church - 49
Sacred Heart Cathedral - 51
Santa Fe Depot - 34
St. Cornelius Episcopal Church - 44
Sughrue Home - 50

National Register Historic Sites

Burr House - 19
Carnegie Arts Center - 25
Downtown Historic District
Hennessy Hall - 78
Home of Stone - 48

Lora-Locke Hotel – 38
Municipal Building - 20
Sacred Heart Cathedral - 51
Santa Fe Depot - 34

National Register Historic Sites, Ford County (outside Dodge City)

Santa Fe Trail Remains - Nine miles west of Dodge City on U.S. 50 - 85
Santa Fe Trail Segment 2 (Fowler's Ruts & Black Pool) - Southwest Corner Ridge Road and
129th Road- 91
Sawlog Creek Crossing on Fort Hays - Fort Dodge Military Road – U.S. 283 and Antelope
Road - 90
Immaculate Heart of Mary Church, Windthorst - fourteen miles east of Wright on Jewell
Road - 91

Register of Historic Kansas Places*

Boot Hill Museum - 9
Hinkle-Heinz House - 58
Kansas Soldiers' Home Cemetery - 88
Kansas Power Company Plant - 62

*All National Register sites are also listed on the Register of Historic Kansas Places

Made in the USA
Columbia, SC
06 September 2020